Elite • 139

Knight's Cross with Diamonds Recipients

1941–45

Gordon Williamson · Illustrated by Ramiro Bujeiro

Consultant editor Martin Windrow

First published in Great Britain in 2006 by Osprey Publishing,
Midland House, West Way, Botley, Oxford OX2 0PH, UK
443 Park Avenue South, New York, NY 10016, USA
Email: **info@ospreypublishing.com**

ISBN 1 84176 644 5

Editor: Martin Windrow
Page layouts by Ken Vail Graphic Design, Cambridge, UK (kvgd.com)
Index by Glyn Sutcliffe
Originated by PPS Grasmere, Leeds, UK
Printed in China through World Print Ltd.

06 07 08 09 10   10 9 8 7 6 5 4 3 2 1

A CIP catalogoue record for this book is available from the British Library

FOR A CATALOGUE OF ALL BOOKS PUBLISHED BY
OSPREY MILITARY AND AVIATION PLEASE CONTACT:

North America:
Osprey Direct
c/o Random House Distribution Center, 400 Hahn Road,
Westminster, MD 21157, USA
Email: **info@ospreydirect.com**

All other regions:
Osprey Direct UK
PO Box 140, Wellingborough, Northants, NN8 2FA, UK
Email: **info@ospreydirect.co.uk**

Buy online at **www.ospreypublishing.com**

Artist's Note

Readers may care to note that the original paintings from
which the colour plates in this book were prepared are
available for private sale. All reproduction copyright
whatsoever is retained by the Publishers. All enquiries
should be addressed to:

Ramiro Bujeiro,
C.C.28,
1602 Florida
Argentina

The Publishers regret that they can enter into no
correspondence upon this matter.

KNIGHT'S CROSS WITH DIAMONDS RECIPIENTS

INTRODUCTION

Due to their immense monetary value, the Oak-Leaves with Swords and Diamonds clasps have frequently been faked. Although the Knight's Cross in this photo is a wartime original, the Diamonds clasp is one of the better quality forgeries which abound, some of which were actually made by the original wartime manufacturers. For photos of genuine pieces, see Plate A.

This decoration was instituted on 28 September 1941 to reward those servicemen who had already been awarded the Oak-Leaves with Swords clasp to the Knight's Cross of the Iron Cross, and had then gone on to distinguish themselves still further. Ultimately, it would be awarded to only 28 of Germany's greatest soldiers, sailors and airmen, ranging from young fighter aces to field marshals.

Description

The first pattern award was based on the design of the standard Oak-Leaves with Swords clasp manufactured by Godet in Berlin, and is the same size as that piece – typically, 27.1mm × 24.6mm. The clasp was drilled out to accept the gemstones, and a strengthening rib was fitted around the reverse edge. These first pattern clasps were awarded to the first few recipients before production was switched to the firm of Klein in the city of Hanau.

The second pattern clasps made by Klein are larger, at around 28mm × 22mm, and are of multi-part construction. The basic clasp is in two parts, with the central leaf being attached to the lower, outer leaf component by two fine rivets; a strengthening rib runs around the reverse edge of the latter. To the base of the clasp are attached two crossed swords, made individually rather than cast as a pair. A long suspension loop completes the clasp. When viewed edge-on the multi-part nature of the construction is clear.

A total of 55 stones were set into the Klein pattern clasp. With this second pattern, two specific types were awarded. The first was the official award made from platinum and set with genuine diamonds. The second set, made from silver and set with facsimile stones, was for wear in service, the risk of damage or loss to the valuable award set being too great for everyday wear.

On the right-hand sword hilt and blade, as viewed from the reverse side, the award pieces bear the metal content mark '950PT' for platinum, as well as the manufacturer's logo of

a letter 'K' within a circle. The crest of Hanau, three chevrons in a circle, is also present. The everyday set was marked similarly, but with '935' for the silver content.

The clasp was presented in a small black leatherette-covered case, with white satin lining to the lid and black velvet covering the base. A length of neck ribbon was also enclosed.

If the award itself is visually impressive, then the award document or Urkunde is spectacular. It was made from vellum and hand lettered, and – unlike the award documents of the preceding classes – in this case the entire text was executed in gold leaf lettering. Held in a leather frame with gold-tooled geometric decoration, it featured the national emblem at the top, followed by the text *Im Namen/des Deutschen Volkes/verleihe ich/dem* [rank]/ [name]/ *das Eichenlaub mit/Schwertern und Brillanten/zum Ritterkreuz/des Eisernen Kreuzes/* [place]/ [date]/ *der Führer/ und Oberste Befehlshaber/ der Wehrmacht*, followed by the signature of Adolf Hitler.

The case in which the document was contained was equally imposing. Covered in morocco leather, it featured a large gilt metal national emblem in the centre and a decorative gilt metal geometric border. These were similar to the fittings on the folder for the Oak-Leaves with Swords document, but in this case the swastika held by the eagle in the national emblem was also set with small diamonds. The leather facings were intended to be in deep red for the Army and Waffen-SS, grey-blue for the Luftwaffe and dark blue for the Kriegsmarine.

THE *BRILLANTENTRÄGER*

Recipients of the Knight's Cross with Oak-Leaves, Swords and Diamonds, in order of date of award of the Diamonds, and in the ranks held at that time:

Oberst Werner Mölders

Werner Mölders was born on 18 March 1913 in Gelsenkirchen. Despite being rejected on his first application to join the Luftwaffe because of air-sickness, he persisted and was eventually accepted. After being commissioned Leutnant he was on flying duties for about a year before being posted as an instructor to the biplane fighter unit Jagdgeschwader 134.

Oberleutnant Mölders came to prominence in the summer of 1938, when he was one of the fighter pilots rotated to Spain – under the guise of individual volunteers – to fly with the Condor Legion supporting Gen Franco's Nationalists in the Civil War.[1] As Staffelkapitän (squadron leader) of 3.Staffel of the fighter group Jagdgruppe 88 in succession to Adolf Galland (qv), flying the early models of the then-revolutionary Messerschmitt Bf 109 monoplane, he became the leading German 'ace' of the war, with 14 confirmed aerial victories. Mölders was instrumental in the development of new fighter tactics based upon small, flexible formations of two and four aircraft – the Rotte and the Schwarm – each pair consisting of a lead pilot with a wingman flying slightly behind and to one side. In a period when most air forces taught pilots to fly in larger formations and to enter combat in a rigid sequence, this new flexibility proved highly successful.

At the outbreak of World War II, Oblt Mölders was Staffelkapitän of 1/JG 53, the lead squadron of the 'Pik As' (Ace of Spades) Geschwader. His first victory of this war came on 21 September 1939, when he shot down a French fighter. Mölders' score continued to rise until 27 May 1940 brought him his 20th victory, the Knight's Cross and promotion to the rank of Hauptmann. Disaster seemed to strike a week later, however, when on 5 June his Bf 109E was shot down by the French ace René Pommier Layragues and he was captured. With a total at that date of 25 victories won during 128 combat missions, it looked as though his flying career was over; but German victory over France brought his release just two weeks later.

Promoted to Major, Mölders was appointed Kommodore of JG 51, and led his wing into the Battle of Britain. On his first patrol over England on 28 July he became involved in a dog-fight with RAF Spitfires of No.74 Sqn led by Sqn Ldr 'Sailor' Malan, whose seventh victim he almost became; three of his Bf 109s were shot down, and he was flying one of three others damaged, being wounded in the legs. Rather than bale out over the Channel, he managed to nurse his damaged Messerschmitt back to Wissant airfield and make an emergency landing.

Mölders went on to achieve considerable success during the Battle of Britain, and on 21 September 1940, when his score had reached 40 kills, he was awarded the Oak-Leaves, as the first Luftwaffe airman to receive this newly created decoration. His tally of victories continued to mount, and in late October he became the first pilot of the war to reach a score of 50 kills,

Hauptmann Werner Mölders, seen here before the award of his Knight's Cross, wears the rare Spanish Gold Cross with Swords and Diamonds for his achievements with the Condor Legion during the Spanish Civil War. Mölders was one of only 27 men to receive this decoration – Adolf Galland was another. Mölders was an honourable and chivalrous man; something of an anachronism in the Third Reich, he was extremely patriotic while making no secret of his dislike of many aspects of National Socialism, which stemmed from his Roman Catholic faith. Even Hitler recognized his qualities, and is recorded as having rounded on some of Mölders' critics among the Nazi leadership and warned them not to harass the Luftwaffe ace, whom Hitler described as a 'decent man'.

ending the year with a total of 55. He remained on the Channel front until the spring of 1941, when JG 51 transferred to the Polish/Russian frontier for the opening of Operation 'Barbarossa'; by this time his score stood at 68 aerial victories.

On 22 June 1941, Mölders was awarded the Swords to his Oak-Leaves with a score of 72, and just a few weeks later he became the first ace to surpass the score of 80 achieved by Baron von Richthofen in World War I. Subsequently he became the first ever to achieve a score of 100 kills, and on 15 July 1941 this brought him the distinction of becoming the first German serviceman to receive the Oak-Leaves with Swords and Diamonds. Reichsmarschall Göring immediately forbade him to fly any further combat missions; and at the age of just 28, Werner Mölders was promoted to the rank of Oberst (full Colonel) and appointed General (or Inspekteur) der Jagdflieger. This was not an executive command, but an appointment with rather ill-defined supervisory duties. He did continue to fly occasional combat sorties despite Göring's orders, however, and achieved several more victories on the Eastern Front which had to remain officially unconfirmed due to the flying ban.

On 22 November 1941, Obst Mölders was on his way back to Germany from an inspection of fighter units at the front, flying as a passenger in a Heinkel He 111 bomber on his way to attend the funeral of Gen Ernst Udet. While attempting a landing at Breslau during a heavy thunderstorm, the Heinkel crashed and Mölders was killed.

Major Mölders as Kommodore of JG 51 on the Channel coast, chatting to Hptm Walter Oesau (right), Kommandeur of his III Gruppe. Mölders displays the Oak-Leaves awarded on 21 September 1940. He was often photographed in fur-collared flying jackets, for which he had acquired a taste during the Spanish Civil War. Oesau would himself win the Oak-Leaves with Swords; he was killed on 11 May 1944 as Geschwaderkommodore of JG 1 in the West, with 71 victories.

Generalleutnant Adolf Galland

Born on 19 March 1912 in Westerholt, Westphalia, to a family of Huguenot blood, Adolf Galland managed to secure a place in a civil flying school in 1932–33, and was one of those pilots who attended clandestine military courses in Germany and Italy. He flew for Deutsche Lufthansa for a short time before volunteering for military service in December 1933. This meant a spell of Army basic training, which Galland carried out with Infanterie Regiment 10 in Dresden. He was discharged in October 1934, and after refresher flying training Lt Galland received his orders in March 1935 to join Jagdgeschwader 2 'Richthofen', the premier fighter unit of the newly revealed Luftwaffe, flying the Heinkel He 51 and Arado Ar 68 biplanes. In October 1935 he crashed an aerobatic Fw 44, suffering serious skull fractures, facial and eye injuries; he only returned to flying with the help of a sympathetic commanding officer who 'lost' his medical records.

In April 1937, Oblt Galland volunteered for the Condor Legion in Spain, and served with 3/J88 flying the He 51. He distinguished himself during many hazardous ground-strafing missions; but despite extending his tour he had to return to Germany before 3.Staffel received the Bf 109, turning his squadron over to the newly arrived Werner Mölders in May 1938. In a staff appointment he helped form the new Schlachtgruppen, and his ground-attack expertise trapped him in such units against his will. As Staffelkapitän of 4.(Schlacht)/LG 2 equipped with Henschel Hs 123 biplanes, Galland flew more than 50 missions during the brief campaign against Poland in September 1939.

In February 1940, during the 'Phoney War' on the Western Front, Galland finally secured a transfer to the staff of a Bf 109 unit, JG 27.

Whenever he could he flew with his friend Mölders of JG 53, building up his hours on the Bf 109E and practising tactics. When the Blitzkrieg was unleashed in May 1940 Galland achieved his first victories on 12 May – three Hurricanes in his first two missions. By the end of the 26-day campaign he had shot down seven Allied aircraft, earning himself the Iron Cross First Class. Neither had his spells of staff work done his reputation any harm; and on 6 June 1940 Hptm Galland arrived with Jagdgeschwader 26 'Schlageter' in the Pas de Calais as Kommandeur of III Gruppe, leading some 30 pilots.

Galland would become famous as one of the leading fighter pilots of the Battle of Britain, and enjoyed meteoric promotion. On 18 July he was promoted to Major, and on the 29th, after scoring his 17th victory, he was awarded the Knight's Cross; on 22 August he was appointed Geschwaderkommodore of JG 26; and on 24 September his 40th victory, bringing his score equal to that of Werner Mölders, earned him the Oak-Leaves. German propaganda presented his friendly rivalry with Mölders as a simplistic race for ever higher kill scores; in fact, both of them were more concerned with the difficulties faced by the pilots of their commands. The Bf 109's short range, Göring's strategic incompetence, his insistence on close bomber escort tactics, and his furious blaming of the fighter pilots for his own mistakes all lowered the morale of the young wing commanders.

When the bulk of the Luftwaffe flew East for the invasion of the USSR in June 1941, JG 2 and JG 26 were left alone to fight the RAF over the Channel and northern France, and soon received the streamlined new Bf 109F. Galland's score and his reputation continued to grow steadily over the months that followed. On 21 June 1941 he became the first serviceman to receive the Swords when his tally reached 70 victories.

Following the accidental death of Werner Mölders on 22 November 1941, Obstlt Galland was appointed to succeed his friend as Inspekteur der Jagdflieger: at the age of 29, he was now directly responsible only to Hermann Göring as Commander-in-Chief of the Luftwaffe. On 5 December 1941, during a leave-taking ceremony at his Geschwader, Galland was promoted to Oberst. Galland's status was enhanced even further when, on 28 January 1942, he was awarded the Diamonds in recognition of his 94 victories – all achieved against first-class opponents on the Western Front, where victories were considered harder to come by than in Russia.

(In his memoirs Galland related that when Göring saw him wearing his newly awarded decoration he inspected it, and insisted that the diamonds were of inferior quality to those commissioned from the jeweller; he denounced this as a fraud, and later personally provided a replacement set with finer stones. Meanwhile Hitler had heard of the incident, and told Galland that the first set had been a temporary measure while the 'proper' diamonds were being prepared; the Führer gave Galland yet another top-quality set, not realising that the set Galland wore were the Göring replacements. Galland thus ended up with multiple sets of the award.)

The Geschwaderkommodore's chevron-and-bar marking dates this photo of Major Galland after 22 August 1940, when he took command of JG 26 – note the 'S for Schlageter' shield ahead of the cockpit. Galland was often pictured wearing these heavy sheepskin trousers from a captured RAF Irvin flying suit. His cigar habit was so strong that he had his ground crew chief fit an electric lighter in the cockpit of his Bf 109.

During 12–15 February 1942, Galland's fighter pilots downed 43 British aircraft for the loss of 17 during cover operations for the successful 'Channel Dash', when the warships *Scharnhorst*, *Gneisenau* and *Prinz Eugen* passed through the English Channel during their transfer from the French port of Brest to Norwegian anchorages. Following this victory, Hitler promoted Galland to the rank of Generalmajor – at the age of 30, the youngest general officer in the German armed forces.

As the war dragged on through 1942–43, and Germany's military fortunes waned on three fronts, Galland tirelessly visited the squadrons in his role as General der Jagdflieger, and communicated their concerns to Göring's Oberkommando der Luftwaffe (OKL); but the weaknesses of the Luftwaffe and the inadequacy of its high command became ever clearer. The flamboyant but ineffectual Göring fell from favour, and as his position weakened he rounded on his air force, looking for scapegoats to blame for his misfortunes. Denied the executive power to put into practice his own clearer-sighted expedients, Galland found himself repeatedly in conflict with OKL. Matters came to a head at a conference early in 1943 when Göring ranted that the fighter pilots were cowards who obtained their decorations by deception. An enraged Galland ripped the Knight's Cross with Oak-Leaves, Swords and Diamonds from his neck and threw it on the table in front of Göring; he refused to wear any of his decorations for fully six months afterwards. In October 1943, Galland unwillingly took under his inspection the Luftwaffe night fighter arm after OKL's dismissal of the able General Kammhuber.

During 1944 the bombing campaign over Germany built into a massive and relentless assault, at the same time as Allied ground offensives in the East and West demanded air cover for the hard-pressed German armies. Battle casualties caused an increasing haemorrhage of experienced fighter pilots (including both of Galland's younger brothers), and their ill-trained replacements had a short life expectancy. Galland – promoted Generalleutnant on 1 November 1944 – spoke up fearlessly against misjudged tactics, and in January 1945 his relations with Göring reached breaking point. Galland had planned a single concentrated operation to hit the US bombers with every fighter the Luftwaffe could scrape up, in the hope of inflicting about 500 losses and massive aircrew casualties, forcing the Allies to rethink their tactics. However, OKL overruled him and used the assembled squadrons – late, wastefully, and for little gain – for an attack on Allied forward airfields on 1 January 1945, in concert with the Ardennes offensive. Relieved of his post as General der Jagdflieger and under threat of Gestapo arrest, Galland contemplated suicide before, at Hitler's personal intervention, he was allowed to return to combat flying.

General Galland visits an airfield in Russia during one of the wartime winters; he wears his usual battered cap, and a sheepskin flying jacket with the pale hide outermost and a dark fleece collar. By the end of 1942 the fighter force, weakened by casualties in Russia, was badly outnumbered over the Mediterranean, and on the Western Front was facing both RAF and USAAF fighter sweeps and the beginnings of the USAAF daylight heavy bomber campaign. Galland was tireless in relaying the concerns of the front-line commanders to the OKL, but had little executive authority himself.

While he was Inspector-General of Fighters, Galland kept up to date by test-flying all new fighter types; and although he had to be discreet, he also flew a number of combat missions. He tried out head-on attacks on US heavy bombers during 1943, shooting down three '*vier-motoren*'; this photo was taken on the day of one of those victories, achieved during a 'familiarization' flight in a Focke-Wulf Fw 190A. Under his life preserver he wears a pale summer-weight flying jacket, his general's breeches with white *Lampassen* stripes, and flying boots. (Private collection)

In late February, Galland took command of the new Jagdverband 44, which was working up with the Me 262 jet fighter; many of its pilots were high-ranking and highly decorated aces, and in the chaotic conditions of Germany's imminent collapse Galland operated more or less independently. In Staffel strength, JV 44 became operational only in early April. Galland scored his last two personal victories – his 103rd and 104th, and his third and fourth in jets – on 26 April; he was wounded, but managed to land in the middle of an attack on Munchen-Reim airfield. On 5 May 1945, GenLt Galland was captured by US forces at Tegernsee hospital.

After his release, Galland spent some years in Argentina, working with the aircraft designer Kurt Tank and introducing jets to the Argentine Air Force. He returned to Germany in 1955, subsequently building a successful career as an aviation businessman. A popular and respected figure, he kept in contact with many wartime airmen, German and Allied, and was particularly friendly with the British ace Wg Cdr Robert Standford Tuck. Adolf Galland died in Bonn on 9 February 1996 at the age of 83.

Oberstleutnant Gordon Gollob

Gordon Gollob was an Austrian, born in Vienna on 16 June 1912. He had Scottish ancestry on his father's side, and his birth name was MacGollob. His military career began when he joined the Austrian army in 1933, transferring to the air force a year later; after qualifying as a pilot he was commissioned Leutnant in 1936. He served as a flying instructor until the Anschluss with Germany in 1938, after which he was taken into the Luftwaffe in the rank of Oberleutnant – he was a convinced supporter of the Nazi regime. It was at this point that he 'Germanicized' his Scottish name to Gollob, but retained 'M' as a middle initial, and continued to be known by his nickname of 'Mac'.

Gollob was in combat from the first day of World War II, flying the twin-engined Messerschmitt Bf 110 'destroyer' heavy fighter with

Zerstörergeschwader 76 in the Polish campaign, during which he gained his first aerial victory. Gollob continued to fly the Bf 110 during the early part of the campaign in the West, shooting down a Sunderland flying boat off Norway, before transferring to Bf 109s as Staffelkapitän of 4/JG 3. After taking part in the Battle of Britain, JG 3 was withdrawn to retrain with the new Bf 109F; they briefly returned to the Channel Front in May 1941, and on 7 May Oblt Gollob achieved his sixth kill. On 27 June he was appointed Gruppen-kommandeur of II/JG 3, shortly before JG 3 was moved East to take part in the invasion of the USSR.

In that 'target-rich environment' Gollob's score really began to take off, and in August 1941 alone he shot down 19 Soviet aircraft. With his score at 42, he was decorated with the Knight's Cross on 18 September 1941. The following month was even more successful: during October he shot down 37 enemy aircraft, including nine on a single day. Just over one month after being decorated with the Knight's Cross, Gollob had raised his score to 85, and on 26 October was awarded the Oak-Leaves. In late November, now promoted to Hauptmann, Gollob was posted away from his unit and assigned to the Luftwaffe test centre at Rechlin, where he was involved in trials of new weapons systems.

Oberst Gordon Gollob, the Austrian former Bf 110 pilot, wearing the Oak-Leaves and Swords with Diamonds awarded at the end of August 1942 when he became the first fighter pilot to achieve 150 victories. Gollob's Scottish ancestry on his father's side, while unusual, was by no means unique in the Wehrmacht: the Luftwaffe also had a fighter ace by the name of Douglas Pitcairn, and the Kriegsmarine an officer named Alistair MacLean.

Returning to the Russian Front in May 1942, Maj Gollob was posted to JG 77 as Kommodore. Operating over the southern sector of the front, he continued to run up an impressive tally of successes over the Crimea. By 20 May he had scored his 100th victory, and by the time this was recognized by the award of the Swords his score had reached 107. On 21 June, Obstlt Friedrich Beckh was posted missing near Kharkov only three weeks after taking command of JG 52, and Gollob was transferred to take over acting command for the next eight weeks. During the month of August 1942 he achieved another 40 victories, more than many good pilots achieved in the entire war. On 29 August 1942 he became the first Luftwaffe fighter pilot credited with 150 kills, an achievement that brought him the Diamonds.

As was normal, the supreme award also meant a transfer away from combat flying, and Gollob was posted as a staff officer to Jagdfliegerführer 5, the fighter headquarters supervising the Channel coast. He remained in staff positions until 1944, ultimately on the Fighter Staff of the Air Ministry. Gollob, although a superb fighter pilot, did not get on well with fellow Diamonds winner Gen Adolf Galland (qv); partly because of the strained relations between the two, Gollob moved back to the Rechlin test unit in September 1944. He led the Jäger Sonderstab, the special staff controlling fighter operations in support of the ill-fated Ardennes offensive in December 1944, when he was criticized for failing to resist the poor judgement of the local theatre GOC, the former bomber commander GenMaj Dietrich Peltz.

When Galland was dismissed as General of Fighters in January 1945 there were spontaneous protests from a group of senior combat commanders – the so-called 'mutiny of the fighter pilots' – and the politically reliable Gollob was appointed to take Galland's place on 31 January 1945, with the rank of Oberst. He held the post until the end of the war.

Gordon Gollob died in retirement at Sulingen on 17 September 1987.

Hauptmann Hans Joachim Marseille

Born in Berlin on 13 December 1919, Marseille had a less than auspicious beginning to what became a dazzling career. Joining I (Jagd)/LG 2 in August 1940, and transferring to 4/JG 52 a few weeks later, he fought during the Battle of Britain as an NCO pilot. He shot down his first Hurricane on 24 August 1940, and before the campaign ended he managed to score six victories; but he achieved this ace status only at the expense of being shot down himself four times, and acquiring a reputation as an insubordinate 'city slicker' who was rather too full of himself. He developed a taste for 'wine, women and song' worthy of Adolf

Hauptmann Marseille
Träger des Eichenlaubs mit Schwertern und Brillanten
zum Ritterkreuz des Eisernen Kreuzes

A wartime propaganda postcard shot of Hans Joachim Marseille; widely lauded in the press, the 'Star of Africa' became a popular public hero – an image no doubt aided by his clean-cut good looks. Although the printed caption describes him as a Hauptmann and bearer of the Knight's Cross with Oak-Leaves, Swords and Diamonds, the photo actually shows him as an Oberleutnant wearing the Oak-Leaves with Swords. It is not thought that Marseille actually received the Diamonds clasp, since he was killed before the presentation could take place.

Galland himself, but without that officer's self-discipline – Marseille was apparently 'too tired' to fly on the morning after some of his wilder excursions into café society. It may have been to get him far from the temptations of occupied France that Oberfähnrich Marseille was posted to I/JG 27, which was designated for service in North Africa.

The Gruppe arrived in Libya in April 1941, still flying the Bf 109E. Marseille's new commanding officer, 'Edu' Neumann, recognized the troublesome ace's great potential as a superb marksman, and encouraged him to practise his skills. Marseille also trained himself gradually to cut down on the use of sunglasses, allowing his eyes to become accustomed to the bright skies over the Western Desert. He soon began to score victories, although shot down himself on 23 April. A lull in operations that summer allowed I/JG 27 to return to Germany to convert to the Bf 109F, of which Marseille would become the unrivalled exponent, always flying aircraft 'yellow 14' with 3 Staffel.

On the single day of 24 September 1941 Marseille shot down five Hurricanes. The Messerschmitt enjoyed a height advantage, and at that time the British and Commonwealth Hurricane and P-40 pilots tended to adopt a defensive circle if attacked. Marseille delighted in the risky tactic of diving at speed to break into the circle, shooting down one or

more aircraft ahead of him while using his skill to turn out of the gunsights of those behind. On 22 February 1942 he was decorated with the Knight's Cross following his 50th victory. His most extraordinary achievement to date came on 6 June 1942, when he attacked a formation of 16 P-40s, and within the space of just 11 minutes shot down six of them, five scored within the first five minutes of the action and two of those within 15 seconds of each other – surviving Allied pilots claimed that they had been attacked by a 'superior enemy force'. Oberleutnant Marseille's feats on that day, which brought his tally to 75 victories, earned him the immediate award of the Oak-Leaves; and just 12 days later, with his score already standing at 101 – all achieved against the RAF – the Swords followed. On 15 June, with 91 victories, he had been promoted to lead 3 Staffel, but he was now sent on two months' leave.

When he returned in the last week of August 1942, Hptm Marseille – at 22, the youngest captain in the Luftwaffe – showed that he had not lost the talent for uncannily accurate deflection shooting and an economy of ammunition that brought him multiple victories in single sorties, even though the Desert Air Force had by now improved markedly in equipment, numbers and skill. During three missions on 1 September 1942 no fewer than 17 aircraft fell to Marseille's guns, and eight of them within just ten minutes of combat; the following day his award of the Diamonds was announced. During the course of September 1942 he added 54 victories to his score, including seven each on the 15th, 26th and 28th of the month; the latter date saw him win his 158th victory, over a Spitfire V. Hauptmann Marseille was promoted, still only 22 years old, to be the youngest major in the Luftwaffe; but the frantic pace of combat flying was visibly exhausting him, and he was shaken by the deaths of his comrades Günther Steinhausen (40 victories) and Hans Arnold Stahlschmidt (59 victories) on 6 and 7 September.

In late September a new Bf 109G fighter was delivered for Marseille. Strongly attached to the trusted old 'Friedrich', he at first refused to fly the new 'Gustav' until ordered to do so by GFM Kesselring (qv) himself. On 30 September he took off for a sweep over Allied territory; no British aircraft were encountered, but on the return flight he reported that his Messerschmitt had developed technical problems. A fractured oil line caused his engine to catch fire, and with his cockpit filling with acrid smoke Marseille had no option but to bale out. Turning his aircraft upside down, he kicked himself free of the cockpit, but as he did so he was struck by the tailplane. With his parachute only partially deployed, Marseille fell to his death.

Oberst Hermann Graf

Born on 24 October 1912 at Engen, Hermann Graf came from a modest background and was no academic star; his poor performance at school seemed to have put an end to his hopes for a career as a military officer. However, he took up sport gliding at the age of 20, and soon gained his glider pilot's licence. He was accepted by the Luftwaffe in 1935, and within a year he had also qualified on powered aircraft. On completing his advanced flying training he was posted to Jagdgeschwader 51 as an NCO pilot in May 1939.

Promoted to Feldwebel just before the outbreak of war, Graf spent his first few months of active service flying uneventful patrols along the French border. In January 1940 he was posted as a flying instructor, a role which took him in October of that year to Romania, where he spent some time with the German military mission training Romanian pilots to fly the Bf 109. In the meantime, in May 1940 he had finally been commissioned Leutnant.

Graf saw combat at last in May 1941, when JG 52 flew ground-attack missions in support of the German airborne invasion of Crete; but it was not to be until 4 August 1941, on the Russian Front, that he would score his first aerial victory. His victim was a Soviet I-16 fighter shot down while 9/JG 52 were flying escort for Ju 87 dive-bombers during an attack on Kiev. By October, Graf had scored 12 kills, and by the end of the year his score had passed 40. On 24 January 1942, Hermann Graf received the Knight's Cross after achieving his 45th victory. On 23 March, by which time his tally had reached 50, Graf was appointed Staffelkapitän of 9/JG 52.

During April 1942 it seemed that Graf could do no wrong, adding a further 48 victories to his score. On 14 May he shot down seven opponents, bringing his total to 104; on the 17th, having reached 106 victories, Graf was awarded the Oak-Leaves, and just two days later the Swords were added – Graf had gained so many victories in such a short time that the award recommendation procedure had problems keeping up with his progress. In the skies over the southern sector of the front, Oblt Graf downed another 32 Soviet aircraft during August 1942 and, incredibly, 62 more during the month of September. On 16 September, with his total at 172 kills, he was awarded the Diamonds;

A fine formal study of Major Hermann Graf, shown here wearing the Diamonds awarded in September 1942, during which month he shot down no fewer than 62 Soviet aircraft. Sadly, after returning from Soviet capitivity he was ostracized by some veterans who believed that he had not shown sufficient defiance to their captors. Graf is believed to have been sickened by witnessing at first hand Nazi atrocities on the Eastern Front, but he nevertheless resisted post-war Soviet pressure to coerce him into joining their puppet East German air force.

on 2 October he became the first fighter pilot ever to have shot down 200 enemy aircraft, and was promoted Hauptmann shortly afterwards. Graf's victories were not easily come by – on one day, his mechanics counted 30 enemy hits on his plane. He was wounded in action in early 1943, and was posted to a training school in France while he recovered.

In the summer of that year, promoted to Major, Graf was tasked with forming and leading JG 50, a new fighter unit to intercept high-flying Allied aircraft, and during his time in this post he downed three USAAF B-17 Flying Fortresses. In November 1943, now with the rank of Oberstleutnant, Graf was appointed as Kommodore of JG 11, a home defence wing. Despite being ordered not to fly combat missions, he continued to add the occasional victory to his tally – six in four months. On 29 March 1944, north of Hanover, he collided with the last of these victims, and was seriously injured while baling out.

Major Graf in the cockpit of a Bf 109, probably when he was serving back in Germany as commander of JG 50; on his left sleeve is the Crimea Shield, awarded for participation in fighter operations over the Crimea in 1941–42. Incidentally, he was also a skilled footballer, who played for the Luftwaffe on many occasions. (Josef Charita)

After recovering, in October 1944 Obstlt Graf returned to the Eastern Front to take command of his old wing; JG 52 was now the only Jagdgeschwader in Russia still equipped with the Bf 109G. Graf would remain in the East throughout the closing seven months of the war, in command of such dazzling aces as Gerhard Barkhorn (see Elite 133), Erich Hartmann (qv) and Günther Rall. At the end of the war, ordered to fly westwards and avoid capture by the Russians, Graf refused to desert his comrades. Although JG 52 eventually managed to surrender to US troops at Pisek on 8 May 1945, they were handed over to the Soviets, and Graf was held in captivity until 1949.

Oberleutnant Graf (centre, with dog) in summer 1942, wearing the Oak-Leaves and Swords as Staffelkapitän of 9/JG 52, flanked by three fellow Ritterkreuzträger among his NCO pilots – Ofw Ernst Süss, Fw Hans Dammers and Ofw Joseph Zwerneman. Of these four, only Graf would survive the war, but between them they would shoot down approximately 480 Allied aircraft.

One of the many propaganda postcards of one of Germany's most popular war heroes, Erwin Rommel. He is pictured here in North Africa, wearing a light olive-brown tropical uniform fitted with regular general officer's rank insignia, and the peaked service cap from the field-grey continental uniform (in 1942, with silver insignia but gold piping and chin cords).

Tragically, in middle age Hermann Graf was struck down by Parkinson's disease; he died on 4 November 1988 at his home town of Engen.

Generalfeldmarschall Erwin Rommel

Erwin Rommel was born at Heidenheim, Württemberg, on 15 November 1891, the son of a schoolmaster. He joined Infanterie Regiment Nr 124 in 1910, and had a distinguished combat career in World War I. After being wounded on the Western Front he transferred in October 1915 to the Württemberg Mountain Battalion, winning the coveted Pour le Mérite ('Blue Max') for conspicuous gallantry in the capture of Italian positions on Monte Matajur in October 1917 during the battle of Caporetto.

He remained in the army between the wars, writing an influential book on infantry tactics; and in 1938, in the rank of Oberst, he was appointed to command Hitler's personal escort battalion. Promoted Generalmajor in June 1939, he took command of 7.Panzer Division in February 1940.

During the invasion of France and the Low Countries in May–June 1940 Rommel excelled as a divisional commander, leading his Panzers from the front as they smashed their way over the Meuse and on to the La Basée Canal. Hitler was delighted with his protégé, and on 26 May 1940 awarded him the Knight's Cross. Rommel ended the campaign at Cherbourg on the Channel coast on 18 June.

In January 1941, Rommel was promoted Generalleutnant; and when Hitler's Italian allies were defeated by the British in North Africa it was Rommel to whom the Führer turned to lead the German expeditionary force that would become the legendary Afrikakorps. German troops began landing in Tripoli in February 1941, and were in action within days, driving the British back. Rommel was recalled briefly to Germany to receive the Oak-Leaves from Hitler on 20 March for his former leadership of 7.Panzer Division. Returning to Africa immediately, Rommel launched a surprise offensive; he failed to take the strategic port of Tobruk, but bypassed it to drive the British back, and destroyed their tank force before lack of supplies forced a halt. He habitually led from the front, which endeared him to his troops and enabled him to exploit opportunities, but sometimes left him dangerously out of touch with the bigger picture. Rommel was promoted General der Panzertruppe on 15 July 1941.

Although forced back to the Gazala line by the British Operation 'Crusader' in November–December, Rommel inflicted massive losses on them; and on 20 January 1942 he received the Swords. His brilliant offensive of May–June 1942 captured Tobruk, and with it over

33,000 Commonwealth troops including five generals. On 22 June a delighted Hitler promoted Rommel to the rank of Generalfeldmarschall – at 50, the youngest in the Wehrmacht – and he became the focus of public adoration. Despite Rommel's successful advance into Egypt at the end of August 1942, however, the situation in North Africa was tipping remorselessly in favour of the British, whose strength was building up, while many of Rommel's vital supply ships from Italy were being sunk by British aircraft and submarines.

On 23 October 1942, while Rommel was on sick leave in Germany, his nemesis, Gen Bernard Montgomery, launched a counter-offensive from the El Alamein line, and maintained the pressure despite heavy casualties. The Italians crumbled, and the Afrikakorps – short of tanks, fuel and supplies – began to falter. By 3 November, Panzerarmee Afrika had only 24 serviceable tanks left, and was forced into a long retreat towards Tunisia. There, caught between the pincers of British 8th Army advancing from the east, and the November landings by British 1st Army and US II Corps in the west, the Italo-German forces were finally crushed in May 1943. Rommel was not allowed to share their fate, however; in March 1943 he was summoned to Hitler's head-quarters to be decorated with the Diamonds, and was immediately sent on sick leave.

Rommel was subsequently appointed C-in-C of Heeresgruppe B in November 1943, and given the task up upgrading the German Atlantic Wall defences against the anticipated Allied invasion attempt – a task into which he threw himself energetically, but in which he was denied the necessary resources and executive authority. When the invasion came on 6 June 1944, Rommel was once again absent on leave; returning to face Montgomery once more, he appealed in vain for the release of reserves to destroy the Allied beachhead. For vital days Hitler and the OKW remained convinced that the Normandy landings were a feint to draw reserves away from the Pas de Calais, and the Allied build-up in the beachhead became unstoppable.

Recognizing the reality, Rommel determined – with the support of senior Waffen-SS commanders such as 'Sepp' Dietrich and Willi Bittrich – to deliver a written memo to Hitler calling on him to conclude a ceasefire in the West; it is believed that if the Führer refused, Rommel had it in mind to surrender the Western Front, to ensure that the British and Americans reached Berlin before the Soviets. The memo was

Rommel with his staff in the Western Desert, 1942, characteristically wearing cellophane British gas goggles on his cap. Strategists may dismiss his style of generalship as risky and opportunist, but Rommel succeeded more often than he failed, and earned both the devotion of his men and the respect of his enemies.

A formal portrait of Generalfeldmarschall Rommel in full field-grey service uniform, wearing – as always – both his Knight's Cross and his Pour le Mérite. Note the silver marshal's crossed baton insignia on his shoulder straps. It was common to have such portraits printed with a space below the image for the subject's signature.

written on 15 July; but on the 17th Rommel's staff car was shot up by a British fighter aircraft and he was seriously injured, sustaining multiple skull fractures.

While Rommel was recuperating the 'bomb plot' attempt was made on Hitler's life on 20 July 1944. When the Gestapo tortured suspects, Rommel's name was mentioned as one of those who favoured the overthrow of the regime – although it seems highly questionable that he knew of the actual assassination plan. On 14 October, Gens Burgdorf and Maisel called at Rommel's home and offered him a choice: he could face the People's Court on charges of treason, with a predictably cruel outcome not just for Rommel but for his family; or he could commit suicide, with the assurance that his family would be spared. Erwin Rommel took the second option, and on the afternoon of that day he took the poison provided by his visitors. The Nazis kept their bargain; Rommel's family went unharmed, and he was given a state funeral after having 'died of his wounds'.

Kapitän zur See Wolfgang Lüth

Wolfgang Lüth was born in the German community in Riga, Estonia, on 15 October 1913. He joined the Navy in 1933, and after commissioning as Leutnant zur See in October 1936 he was posted to the U-boat service. He learned his trade as a watch officer under experienced commanders in U-27 and U-38; and in December 1939 ObltzS Lüth was given his own command, the Type IIB boat U-9. During his six months as captain of this small coastal boat he sank an Allied submarine and damaged a destroyer.

In June 1940, Lüth took over a Type IID, U-138; during two war cruises in the Atlantic he sank a total of nearly 40,000 tons of shipping, bringing him the Knight's Cross on 24 October 1940. In the same month Lüth was posted to command U-43, an ocean-going Type IXA, in which he completed six war cruises in the Atlantic, adding a further nine ships to his tally and taking his total to 54,800 tons.

In May 1942, Lüth was given command of U-181, a long-range Type IXD. With this boat he embarked on his first cruise into the South Atlantic, around the Cape of Good Hope and into the waters of the Indian Ocean. There he sank 12 Allied ships totalling over 58,000 tons during 128 days at sea; and on 13 November 1942, Lüth's achievements brought him the Oak-Leaves.

In March 1943 Lüth took U-181 out again on a cruise which was to set a new record, lasting a total of 205 days. His area of operations was again to be the Indian Ocean and in particular the waters around Mauritius. In these seas there were none of the large convoys that were

to be found in the Atlantic, and U-181 was forced to hunt for single merchantmen. While on this patrol, on 1 April 1943 Lüth was promoted to Korvettenkapitän, and on 15 April he received a signal announcing that he had been awarded the Swords. When U-181 finally reached Bordeaux after her return voyage, she had sunk ten ships for a total of 45,000 tons. His record of 105,812 tons during his two Indian Ocean cruises brought Lüth promotion to Fregattenkapitän on 1 August, and the Diamonds on 9 August 1943. His career record of 46 ships sunk with a total displacement of 228,429 GRT was second only to that of Korvettenkapitän 'Silent Otto' Kretschmer, whose 43 sinkings totalled 263,682 tons.

On 1 January 1944, Lüth was posted as commander of 22.U-Flotille; he would not go to sea again. In July 1944 he was posted to the Marineschule at Mürwick and took command of the establishment in September of that year, with the rank of Kapitän zur See. He remained in this position until the end of the war. Ironically, after surviving prolonged service in one of the most dangerous branches of the armed forces, and receiving the highest of military decorations, Wolfgang Lüth would die at the hands of one of his own men a week after the war had ended. On the evening of 14 May 1945 he was taking a stroll around the grounds of the academy when he was challenged by a nervous German sentry; his mind presumably on other things, he failed to respond, and the sentry shot him dead.

Major Walter Nowotny

Born in Gmund, Austria, on 7 December 1920, Walter Nowotny volunteered for the Luftwaffe and reported for duty on 1 October 1939. After pilot training he was posted to Breslau-Schogarten, where he flew fighter cover for the Leuna industrial works. Shortly afterwards he was

A cheerful-looking Hauptmann Walter Nowotny, in a portrait taken just after the award of the Diamonds on 19 October 1943 for his 250th kill. As the Kommandeur of I/JG 54 'Grünherz' flying Fw 190s on the Russian Front this Austrian pilot had achieved a dazzling record, on more than one occasion shooting down ten Soviet aircraft in the course of a single day.

assigned to JG 54 'Grünherz' under the command of Maj Hannes Trautloft.

Promoted Leutnant on 1 April 1941, Nowotny scored his first three kills during a single mission with 9/JG 54 on 19 July of that year, when JG 54 was assigned to the northern Russian Front. His Bf 109F was damaged by the third Polikarpov, and he had to ditch in the Baltic near the island of Ösel; he spent two days and nights in his dinghy before reaching shore and being rescued. (Thereafter he always flew in his patched, salt-stained breeches – his lucky 'Shot-down Trousers'.) By August 1941 his score had passed ten, bringing him the Iron Cross First Class.

The 'Green Heart' wing settled in on airfields in the Leningrad sector, and victories now began to come rapidly; on 14 September 1941, with his score at 56, Nowotny was awarded the Knight's Cross, and he took over leadership of 1/JG 54 on 25 October. Hauptmann Hans Philipp's I Gruppe were then progressively rotated back to Heiligenbeil in East Prussia to convert on to the Focke-Wulf Fw 190A, and Nowotny was back at Krasnogvareisk airfield with his new mount in November.

It was in summer 1943 that Oblt Nowotny really began to stand out from the list of successful fighter pilots. During June he achieved 41 victories, scoring his 100th on 15 June and ten in the single day of 24 June. On 5 July, I Gruppe were transferred south to operate on the northern flank of the Kursk salient during Operation 'Citadel'. There Nowotny would be lucky to survive: the Gruppe would lose six pilots, including their Kommandeur, Maj Reinhard Seiler, wounded on 6 July. On 3 August his replacement, Maj Gerhard Homuth, was lost, and Homuth's acting replacement, 2/JG 54 Staffelkapitän Hans Götz, fell the following day. The Gruppe was forced north once again by the Soviet counter-offensive which followed the failure of the Kursk operation, being shuttled up and down the front like a fire brigade; but from this grim period for his unit Walter Nowotny's record would shine out.

In August 1943, Oblt Nowotny shot down 49 Soviet aircraft, and on 21 August he was promoted Gruppenkommandeur of I/JG 54. On 1 September he again recorded ten kills in a single day, including seven in just 17 minutes. On the 4th, when his score stood at 191, he was awarded the Oak-Leaves. By the time he reported to Rastenburg to receive the clasp, on 22 September, his score had reached 220; this brought him the Swords at the same investiture ceremony and made him, at that time, the highest-scoring pilot in the world. By 14 October, promoted Hauptmann, Nowotny had taken his tally to 250 victories – once again, a record-breaking first; and on the 19th of that month he was awarded the Diamonds (the phone call from the Führer reached him in the

middle of a party in a bar in Vilnius, Lithuania). Nowotny's 255th and final victory on the Eastern Front came on 15 November 1943; thereafter it was ordered that as a holder of the Diamonds he cease to fly combat sorties. He was transferred to a non-combatant post as commander of a flying training school, JG 101, based at Paux, France.

In September 1944 Hitler finally relaxed his nonsensical ban on the use of the revolutionary Me 262 jet in the fighter role, and Gen Galland (qv) immediately began trying to reorganize the small test units to serve the needs of the home defence force. Galland formed one jet Einsatzkommando at the adjoining Achmer and Hesepe airfields near Osnabrück, and on 20 September Maj Nowotny took command of the two-Staffel unit which was to bear his name. Two pilots of Kommando Nowotny flew the first combat mission from Hesepe on 7 October, shooting down two B-24s; but three trying to take off from Achmer were 'bounced' by Mustangs, and thereafter the Fw 190Ds of 9/ and 10/JG 54 were brought in to fly standing patrols for jets taking off or landing. A series of accidents and technical failures stopped operational flying from 13 to 28 October. Thereafter victories and losses continued, in small numbers – the unit was dogged by the technical unreliability of the Me 262's engines.

On 8 November 1944, when Gens Galland and Keller were due to visit, Nowotny scheduled missions by two machines each from Achmer and Hesepe, intending to fly his own first jet combat mission in one of the former. That morning his engines failed to start, and only two jets got off to engage the approaching USAAF bombers. That afternoon Nowotny took off with Lt Franz Schall to intercept the returning bomber stream. Disappearing into unbroken cloud, Nowotny later radioed that he had shot down a bomber and possibly a P-51; then he reported engine failure. Under Galland's appalled eyes, Nowotny's jet plunged vertically out of the clouds. All that could be recovered were minimal human remains, and his Knight's Cross with Oak-Leaves, Swords and Diamonds.

Mechanics working on 'white 4', an Me 262A-1a twin jet fighter of Kommando Nowotny, at Achmer airfield in late September 1944. Nowotny's impatient efforts to get his squadron operational were dogged by the Me 262's unreliability, and the shortage of two-seat trainers.

At Nowotny's state funeral in Vienna, Gordon Gollob holds the *Ordenskissen* – a black velvet cushion with the dead man's decorations. Gollob wears both the Narvikand Crimea shields on his sleeve.

Generalmajor Adalbert Schulz, shown here in his black Panzer uniform, wears the Oak-Leaves with Swords and Diamonds awarded in December 1943 for his leadership as colonel commanding Pz Regt 25; he was promoted Generalmajor at the beginning of January 1944, but was dead of wounds less than a month later. Here the all-ranks' death's-head collar patches of the black 'special uniform' can be seen; another photo shows Schulz wearing on the black jacket – against regulations – the standard gold-on-red generals' 'Alt Larisch' patches from the service uniform. It is interesting that of the 11 Army officers who received the Diamonds, no fewer than four – Rommel, Schulz, Manteuffel and Mauss – had served with 7.Panzer Division.

Oberst Adalbert Schulz

Adalbert Schulz was born in Berlin on 20 December 1903. After service with the Police he transferred into the Wehrmacht in 1935, with the rank of Oberleutnant. In 1938, Schulz was given command of 1 Kompanie of Panzer Regiment 5, in 7.Pz Div, where he gained promotion to Hauptmann.

During the 1940 campaign in the West, Hptm Schulz distinguished himself in the capture of fiercely defended French positions in the forest of Saumont, and held them against numerous counter-attacks mounted with armoured support. So great was the impression that Schulz made on his superiors that he was recommended for the Iron Crosses in both classes as well as the Knight's Cross, all at the same time. The awards were approved on 29 September 1940.

Promoted to battalion command, he took over I/Pz Regt 25, and led this unit during the invasion of the Soviet Union in summer 1941. Schulz once again distinguished himself during these fast-moving actions, achieving victories at the Minsk pocket, the Dnieper crossings, Smolensk and on the approaches to Moscow. His recommendation for the Oak-Leaves was approved on 31 December 1941. In winter 1941/42 Schulz took part in costly defensive fighting around Rzhev before his division was withdrawn to France for rest and refitting in May 1942.

Over the winter of 1942/43, 7.Pz Div returned to the Eastern Front and was thrown into action on the Donetz under Heeresgruppe Süd in the face of the Soviet counter-offensives following the fall of Stalingrad. On 11 March 1943, during the defence of Kharkov, Schulz took part in fierce engagements against Soviet armour during one of which his Panzers destroyed over 100 enemy tanks and many artillery pieces. Schulz was promoted to Oberstleutnant on 1 April 1943, taking command of his regiment. In early July he led Pz Regt 25 in Operation 'Citadel', the great armoured offensive around Kursk, once more displaying great courage and elan in actions at Belgorod, Dorogobushino, Scheino and Prokhorovka. On 6 August 1943 he was awarded the Swords.

Schulz was promoted to Oberst on 1 November 1943. In the fierce defensive fighting around Kiev and Zhitomir, Pz Regt 25 carried out surprise attacks on the flanks of advancing enemy formations, destroying more than 150 Soviet tanks and checking the advance. For this, as well as his distinguished leadership of the regiment over the preceding months, Schulz was awarded the Diamonds on 14 December 1943. Ordered to travel to Hitler's headquarters to receive the award in person, Schulz refused the invitation until he was satisfied that the situation on his sector of the front was stable enough to allow him to leave. Schulz was promoted to Generalmajor on 1 January 1944, and took command of 7.Panzer Division.

On 28 January 1944, GenMaj Schulz was conducting a battlefield command conference next to his tank during an attack on Shepetovka when he was seriously wounded by a nearby shellburst. Immediately evacuated to hospital, he died of his wounds before he could be treated.

Oberst Hans Ulrich Rudel

Hans Ulrich Rudel was born on 2 July 1916 at Konradswaldau, the son of a clergyman. At school his academic success was mediocre, his real passion being for sport. Nevertheless, he was accepted into the Luftwaffe in 1936 as an officer cadet, and after completing flying training was duly commissioned Leutnant. He flew reconnaissance missions during the Polish campaign, winning the Iron Cross Second Class, before requesting a transfer to dive-bombers in May 1940. He missed the campaign in France and the Low Countries while he undertook conversion training on to the Junkers Ju 87B.

Rudel's first combat mission as a Stuka pilot, with 1 Staffel of Stukageschwader 2 'Immelmann', was flown in May 1941 during the attacks on Crete. He was soon in action again, as late June saw I/ and III/StG 2 taking part in the invasion of the Soviet Union. After several successful missions, Lt Rudel was awarded the Iron Cross First Class on 18 July. On 23 September 1941, flying from Tyrkovo, the two Gruppen of StG 2 mounted an attack on the Soviet naval harbour at Kronstadt. Rudel dropped his 1,000kg bomb from a 90° dive, hitting the battleship *Marat;* her magazine exploded, breaking her back, and she sank at her anchorage. By 24 December 1941, Rudel had flown 500 combat missions, and on the 30th of the month he was awarded the German Cross in Gold. Withdrawn to Germany for a brief spell as an instructor, on 15 January 1942 he was awarded the Knight's Cross, a recommendation for which had been initiated after his sinking of the *Marat.*

A fine portrait showing Major Rudel's Oak-Leaves, Swords and Diamonds to good effect. Clasps in both the original silver and the unique gold versions remain in the possession of his family to this day.

After returning to the Eastern Front as a Staffelkapitän with III Gruppe of the retitled Schlachtgeschwader 2, Rudel kept up a punishing pace of operations throughout most of the vast ground campaigns on that front; 1942 saw SG 2 re-equipped with the improved Ju 87D model of the Stuka. By February 1943, after Rudel had flown his 1000th dive-bomber mission, he was given the opportunity to help develop a new version of the Stuka armed with two long 3.7cm cannon slung under the wings in pods; the slow, unmanoeuvrable Stuka was becoming painfully outclassed, and a new ground-attack mission would be more valuable than its traditional dive-bomber role. Rudel tested the new aircraft in attacks on Soviet landing craft in the Black Sea, and in three weeks of operations he was credited with sinking 70 of them. Subsequent operations against enemy tanks in March 1943 proved equally successful; and by 14 April, when he was awarded the Oak-Leaves, Hptm Rudel was Gruppenkommandeur of III/SG 2.

During the massive tank battles of the Kursk offensive Rudel began to run up a considerable tally of enemy armour destroyed by gunfire; on the first day of the campaign alone, 5 July 1943, he destroyed 12 Soviet tanks. On 25 October 1943 the Swords were added to his Oak-Leaves; and by March 1944, with more than 1,500 combat missions in his logbooks, he was promoted to Major. During that month, when one of his pilots was shot down behind enemy lines, Rudel landed his own aircraft in an attempt to rescue him, only to find the ground too soft and marshy to allow him to take off again. Forced to destroy his aircraft,

As well as the Knight's Cross with Oak-Leaves, Swords and Diamonds, in this photo Hans Ulrich Rudel can be seen to wear, in addition to his regular Pilot's Badge, the Pilot/Observer badge with Diamonds which was in Göring's personal gift (he also presented it to Mölders and Galland). Rudel also wears a diamond-studded Front Flight Clasp awarded after his 2,000th mission. (Josef Charita)

Rudel and his comrades made their way across country pursued by Soviet troops, finally swimming the icy waters of the 600-yard wide River Dniestr to reach German-held territory. Tragically, Rudel's rear gunner drowned during the crossing, the two airmen he was attempting to rescue were cut down by enemy gunfire, and Rudel himself was wounded. This was only one of six occasions on which Rudel risked his life to land behind enemy lines to rescue shot-down comrades.

On his return, on 29 March 1944, Rudel was decorated with the Diamonds for his gallantry. He continued to fly anti-tank missions; and on 1 January 1945, Rudel was awarded the Golden Oak-Leaves with Swords and Diamonds – as the only recipient of this unique award – and promoted to the rank of Oberst. Badly shot up by enemy flak in February

Rudel (left) photographed with Fw Bölling and Uffz Maldinger, two veteran members of his Stuka group. (Private collection)

The type of aircraft in which Rudel achieved his extraordinary successes against Soviet tanks: the Junkers Ju 87G, a D-model with two long-barrelled 3.7cm cannon in pods attached under the wings, with horizontal automatic-feed magazines. Although obsolete as an anti-tank gun in ground combat, the 3.7cm was highly effective against the thinner top armour of Soviet tanks. (Private collection)

1945, Rudel had to have a leg amputated; but despite this he was back in the cockpit of his Ju 87G flying combat missions before the end of the war, adding a further 13 enemy tanks to his score. Generalfeldmarschall Schörner said of him that 'Rudel alone is worth an entire division', and his record shows that this was not much of an exaggeration: by the end of the war he had flown more than 2,500 combat missions, in the course of which he had sunk one battleship, two cruisers, a destroyer and 70 landing craft, and had destroyed 519 tanks, 70 artillery pieces, 1,000-plus sundry other vehicles, and 11 enemy aircraft.

Rudel went into US captivity on 8 May 1945. A convinced and unrepentant Nazi, he lived for a time in South America. He eventually returned to Germany, where he was active in radical right-wing circles. He died on 18 December 1982.

A Panzer officer who seems to have worn the special black uniform whenever possible, Hyazinth Graf Strachwitz is seen here after the award of the Swords, earned in command of Pz Regt 2 in 16.Pz Div on the advance to Stalingrad. He is wearing his unique fleece-trimmed version of the Panzer officer's field cap (see Plate D). Count Strachwitz was wounded 13 times in all, and his overall health suffered badly during his time on the Eastern Front. It is reported that he would be found in his armoured vehicle unable to walk, blinded by headaches and barely conscious, but refusing to be evacuated for treatment.

Generalmajor Hyazinth Graf Strachwitz

Born on 30 July 1893 in Grosstein Castle, Strachwitz came from an old family of the Silesian nobility (his full style was Hyazinth Graf Strachwitz von Gross-Zauche und Camminetz). He served with distinction, if briefly, as a cavalry subaltern in the opening weeks of World War I, winning both classes of the Iron Cross before being captured by the French in September 1914, and eventually returning to Germany only in 1918.

By the outbreak of World War II, Count Strachwitz was a Hauptmann with Panzer Regiment 2 in 1.Pz Div, with which unit he served during the campaign in Poland. During the attack on France in 1940, 1.Pz Div was initially part of Panzergruppe von Kleist, advancing through Luxemburg and the Ardennes to Sedan, before being transferred to Panzergruppe Guderian on 10 June. In one incident, Strachwitz and one of his junior officers stumbled upon a French signals unit in barracks; he bluffed the French commander – baffled at seeing Germans so deep behind his own lines – into surrendering his 600 men, mounting them in their own vehicles, and accompanying Strachwitz back to his unit and captivity. This was typical of Strachwitz's 'light cavalry' style; and in recognition of his daring he was promoted to Major. In late October 1940, Pz Regt 2 was transferred to form the cadre of the newly raised 16.Pz Div, which moved to Romania on a training mission in December.

During the opening phases of Operation 'Barbarossa' from June 1941, 16.Pz Div served with Heeresgruppe Süd as part of Gen Hube's (qv) XIV Panzerkorps in Kleist's 1.Panzergruppe. The division fought in all the major victories of this slashing advance; Strachwitz continued to prove himself as an audacious and resourceful combat officer, and on 25 August 1941, after the closing of the Uman pocket, he was awarded the Knight's Cross. The division fought at Kremenchug in the southern pincer of the vast encirclement around Kiev in September, before plunging on towards the Don, eventually being driven back from the Rostov salient in December 1941. After hard defensive fighting in the winter, Obstlt Strachwitz, now commanding Pz Regt 2, led his tanks in the forefront of the summer 1942 advance to the Don and across it to Stalingrad; at Kalach on the Don his regiment destroyed more than 270 Soviet tanks within 48 hours. In October the division was the first to reach the Volga north of Stalingrad; but Strachwitz's age of 49, and the effect of the latest of his many wounds, led to his being evacuated before the Soviet ring closed around the city, and he thus escaped the annihilation of 16.Panzer Division. During his recuperation he was awarded the Oak-Leaves on 13 November 1942.

On his recovery in January 1943 he was promoted Oberst and posted to command the Panzer regiment of Gen Walter Hoernlein's elite 'Grossdeutschland' Division, which was being rebuilt near Smolensk after disastrous casualties east of Rzhev during the Soviet winter offensive. It was soon back in the line, fighting around Belgorod and Kharkov in February and March 1943. Particularly heavy combat around the villages of Borisovka and Tomarovka brought Strachwitz the award of the Swords on 28 March. On one occasion, with just four Panzers of his own, he ambushed and destroyed 105 Soviet tanks in little over 30 minutes; on another, after his regiment had received a battalion of Tiger heavy tanks, these destroyed 100 enemy tanks in just one hour of combat. Count

Strachwitz, the 'Panzer Cavalier', was a soldier's soldier who was usually in the thick of the action with his men – a habit that he retained not merely as a battalion and regimental commander, but even when he rose to general rank.

After refitting in April–May 1943, in July the newly retitled PzGren Div 'Grossdeutschland' fought under GenObst Hoth's 4.Panzerarmee in the southern pincer of the Kursk offensive. The lavishly equipped 'GD' had some 300 tanks when it advanced into the deep Soviet defensive lines north of Belgorod on 5 July; but after early success it was halted on the Oboyan heights on the 9th, and on the 12th the reverse suffered by Hausser's SS-Panzerkorps on the division's right flank doomed the offensive. In August and September, Strachwitz's Panzers fought dispersed in fierce defensive battles west of Kharkov, and by 29 September he had just one operational tank left. Pushed back across the Dniepr, by late December the 'GD' was far to the west at Kirovgrad.

Still part of 4.Panzerarmee, the rebuilt division – now commanded by Gen Hasso von Manteuffel (qv) – fought as a fire brigade in a number of threatened sectors in early 1944. In April, when the port of Riga on the Baltic coast was completely surrounded, Strachwitz personally led a relief attack from the turret of one of the leading tanks, and successfully broke through the enemy encirclement to rescue the German garrison, which included huge numbers of wounded. For this achievement, on 15 April 1944 he was awarded the Diamonds and promoted to Generalmajor.

Not long afterwards GenMaj Strachwitz was almost killed in a traffic accident. Despite severe injuries, and walking on crutches, he discharged himself and reported back 'fit for duty'. Promoted to Generalleutnant on 1 January 1945, he spent the last months of the war commanding an anti-tank brigade on the Eastern Front, still inflicting maximum losses on the enemy with the minimum of fast-moving mobile forces. He finally surrendered to US troops in May 1945.

After the war Strachwitz spent some time in Syria before returning to Germany in 1951. Hyazinth Graf Strachwitz died in retirement on 25 April 1968, and was one of the few senior commanders under the Third Reich to be buried with full military honours in the post-war years.

A fuller portrait of Oberst Graf Strachwitz shows his other awards from both World Wars: Iron Cross First Class with the silver eagle clasp showing that it had also been awarded in World War I, Tank Battle Badge, and Wound Badge in Gold for five or more wounds. Note also on his right forearm the cuff band of the 'Grossdeutschland' Division, whose Panzer regiment he commanded in 1943–44.

SS-Gruppenführer u. Generalleutnant der Waffen-SS Herbert Otto Gille

Herbert Otto Gille was born at Gandersheim on 8 March 1897. Service in the artillery in World War I left him with both classes of the Iron Cross, but no career. After 15 years as a civilian he joined the SS-Verfügungstruppe (SS-VT) in 1934, working his way up through platoon, company and battalion command positions in SS-Regt 'Germania'. In the spring of 1939 Gille, now an SS-Obersturmbannführer (lieutenant-

In this photo SS-Gruf Herbert Otto Gille can clearly be seen to wear the second pattern Klein-made Diamonds clasp he was awarded on 19 April 1944.

colonel), was posted to assist in the formation of a new artillery regiment for the SS-VT, and became one of its battalion commanders. In this post he took part in both the Polish and French campaigns.

It was to be on the Eastern Front, however, that Gille was to come to the fore. Having moved from the SS-Verfügungs Div (later 'Das Reich') to take command of the artillery regiment of the newly formed multinational SS-Div 'Wiking', Gille led his troops with considerable elan and personal courage in the invasion of the Soviet Union, when the division formed part of III, and later XIV Panzerkorps in Heeresgruppe Süd. It fought at Tarnopol, Uman and Korsun before halting on the Mius line during winter of 1941/42; and in 1942 it advanced deep into the Caucasus, reaching the Terek river. On 8 October 1942, SS-Oberführer Gille was rewarded with the Knight's Cross.

In May 1943, Gille was appointed to command the newly upgraded SS-PzGren Div 'Wiking' with the rank of SS-Brigadeführer (major-general). Under Gille's leadership 'Wiking' continued to build on its reputation for aggressiveness in the assault and steadfastness in defence. In October 1943 the division was again upgraded to become the first 'Germanic' (i.e. partly non-German) Panzer division of the Waffen-SS, and spent the latter part of the year fighting in the Ukraine. On 1 November 1943, Gille was awarded the Oak-Leaves for his command of the division.

In January 1944, 5.SS-Pz Div 'Wiking' was trapped in the Cherkassy Pocket with five other German divisions, surrounded by 35 Soviet divisions. After the pocket had been squeezed down to an area of about 38 square miles, Hitler – unusually – gave permission for a break-out. Led by 'Wiking', the attempt was successful, saving 34,000 out of the 55,000 troops who had been trapped. For this achievement Gille was awarded the Swords on 20 February 1944.

Gille's greatest test came that spring, when Hitler ordered him to take the exhausted remnant of his division to hold the 'fortress' town of Kovel – the last German bastion east of the 1939 Polish border – against an impending encirclement by four complete Soviet armies. Gille knew that this was a suicide mission, and insisted on a personal audience with Hitler. This was denied him; but he still refused to take his remaining troops into Kovel, and instead flew into the pocket alone. Here, with no anti-tank guns, he led the beleaguered garrison's resistance until a handful of tanks from 'Wiking' managed to break into the pocket. With this small but vital addition to his defensive capabilities, Gille held out for another eight days, until the rest of his division plus two other Panzer divisions and an infantry division broke through to relieve them. For this astonishing achievement, on 19 April 1944 he was awarded the Diamonds.

Gille was then tasked with forming IV SS-Panzerkorps, and this formation (with 3.SS-PzDiv 'Totenkopf' and 5.SS-PzDiv 'Wiking') saw action in the defensive battles around Warsaw from August 1944. On 9 November 1944, Gille was promoted to SS-Obergruppenführer (full general); and the following month his corps was thrown into the doomed attempt to halt the Soviet advance into Hungary. Forced back into Austria in the closing stages of the war, Gille surrendered to US forces at Radstadt in May 1945.

He lived in retirement and near-poverty in Germany for many years, but never lost touch with his former soldiers, and was responsible for setting up the newsletter of the Waffen-SS veterans association (HIAG). Gille died suddenly of a heart attack on 26 December 1966.

Generaloberst Hans Hube

Hans Valentin Hube was born at Naumburg on 29 October 1890. At 18 years of age he joined Infanterie Regiment Nr 26 'Fürst Leopold von Anhalt-Dessau' in Magdeburg as an officer cadet, and in 1910 was commissioned Leutnant. He fought as a platoon commander and battalion adjutant in the first month of World War I, but was badly wounded at Fontenay, losing his left arm. Nevertheless, he returned to combat duty with his regiment in January 1916. In 1918, after being caught in a British gas attack, he was recommended for the Pour le Mérite for his conduct, but the war ended before this could be approved. In October 1919, Hube joined the Reichswehr of the new Weimar Republic, and thereafter served variously as a company commander, battalion commander, staff officer, and instructor at Döberitz military school, where he published his well-received two-volume work *Der Infanterist.*

In October 1939, Obst Hube was posted to command Inf Regt 3, which he led until he was promoted Generalmajor in May 1940 to take command of 16.Inf Div (mot), which was soon re-organized to become 16.Panzer Division. Hube then balanced command of this division with additional duties as commander of the German training staff in Romania.

Hube performed with distinction in the opening phases of Operation 'Barbarossa' with Heeresgruppe Süd (see under Graf Strachwitz, above). He led his division to victory at Starya-Konstatynov against numerically superior enemy forces and beat off counter-attacks, winning the Knight's Cross on 7 July 1941. The award of the Oak-Leaves followed on 16 January 1942 for his distinguished leadership in the winter defensive battles around Nikolayev and Kiev. Hube was promoted to Generalleutnant on 15 September 1942, and appointed to command XIV Panzerkorps. On 21 December of that year he was awarded the Swords for his command of the corps during the thrust to the Volga north of Stalingrad. Hube was flown out of the encirclement for the award ceremony, but returned immediately afterwards. On Hitler's orders, however, he was flown out once again on 18 January 1943; he pleaded in vain with the Führer to allow 6.Armee to break out of the encirclement, but his corps was annihilated in the final collapse at Stalingrad.

In March 1943, GenLt Hube was tasked with rebuilding XIV Panzerkorps, before being posted in July to Sicily, where he commanded all Army and Flak troops on the island. He fought with great skill and determination in Sicily and on the Italian mainland that summer, though he was unable to crush the Salerno landings. In late October 1943, Hube was placed on the leadership reserve of the Army High Command (OKH); but in mid-February 1944 he was posted East once more to take command of 1.Panzerarmee under Heeresgruppe Süd in the Dniepr

The one-armed combat veteran of World War I, Hans Valentin Hube, was popularly known as 'Clever Hans'. He was killed in an air crash on his return from investiture with the Diamonds, awarded in April 1944 for his skilful leadership in Sicily, Italy and the Korsun Pocket in southern Russia. In this photo he wears the standard Oak-Leaves with Swords.

bend. Hube was responsible for breaking out of the Korsun Pocket towards Kamanetz-Podolsk in late March–early April 1944. On 1 April he was promoted to Generaloberst; and three weeks later, for his distinguished leadership in Sicily, Italy and at Korsun, Hube was awarded the Diamonds.

The ceremony took place at Hitler's headquarters at the Obersalzberg on 20 April 1944; the following day, as Hube set off on his return journey to the front, the Heinkel He 111 in which he was travelling crashed, and Hube was killed.

Generalfeldmarschall Albert Kesselring

Albert Kesselring was born on 30 November 1885 at Marksteft near Kitzingen, the son of a schoolmaster. In the summer of 1904 he joined the Bavarian foot artillery as an officer cadet, and was commissioned Leutnant in 1907; by the outbreak of war in 1914 he had been promoted to Oberleutnant. He served throughout World War I with Bavarian artillery units and in staff positions. He remained in the post-war Army, serving in regimental and senior staff appointments and rising to the rank of Oberst in 1932. On 1 October 1933, Kesselring was officially discharged from the Army to become a civilian official with the State Commission for Air Transport – a cover organization for the creation of the clandestine Luftwaffe. In March 1935, when the existence of the Luftwaffe was proclaimed, Kesselring was appointed Chief of the Administration Department at the Air Ministry with the rank of Generalmajor.

Promotion to Generalleutnant followed in April 1936 when he was appointed Chief of the Luftwaffe General Staff. On 1 June 1937 he was promoted General der Flieger and appointed commander of Air District III in Dresden, moving the following year to Luftwaffen Kommando I in Berlin; this later became Luftflotte 1. He commanded this major formation – the equivalent of an army – during the invasion of Poland, and was rewarded with the Knight's Cross on 30 September 1939. He then took command of Luftflotte 2; he worked hard to perfect ground-air co-operation for the Blitzkrieg campaigns, and on 19 July 1940, after the successful conclusion of the campaign in the West, Kesselring was promoted to Generalfeldmarschall.

Allocated to the support of Heeresgruppe Mitte, Luftflotte 2 repeated its success in 1941 during the first four months of the invasion of the Soviet Union. That October it was transferred to the Mediterranean and North Africa, with GFM Kesselring taking overall command of German forces in that theatre in December 1941 as Oberbefehlshaber Süd, based in Rome – a notable compliment to an air force officer. He was more patiently diplomatic than most German senior officers in his often difficult dealings with the Italian High Command. Kesselring was awarded the Oak-Leaves on 25 February 1942, and the Swords on 18 July of the same year, at the high point of the Axis advance in North Africa. He had urged the invasion of Malta in April 1942, but Hitler rejected the plan; Kesselring was ultimately unable to provide adequate air cover for the Afrikakorps or to keep Rommel (qv) supplied.

After the Allied landings in Sicily in July 1943 and the successful withdrawal of much of the garrison to the mainland, Kesselring was appointed Oberbefehlshaber Süd-West and Heeresgruppe C (10. & 14.Armee) for the defence of Italy. It was this campaign that gave him the chance to show his real brilliance, and for which, on 19 July 1944, he was decorated with the Diamonds. Outnumbered, but blessed by holding excellent ground for defence, he reacted to each Allied initiative with great speed and skill. He repeatedly extracted his troops from danger at the last minute, only to instal them in defences further north, forcing the Allied generals to undertake a series of costly assaults which never succeeded in trapping the German defenders.

During an inspection visit to the front in October 1944, GFM Kesselring was injured in a car crash, and did not return to active duty for some months. On 9 March 1945 he was appointed Oberbefehlshaber der Westfront in succession to Rundstedt, at a point when the war was already hopelessly lost. At the end of April he was again made C-in-C South, and was only reluctantly forced to accept the German surrender on this front negotiated by other senior officers.

On 6 May 1947 Kesselring was sentenced to death on charges relating to war crimes against Italian civilians by SS troops under his theatre command. The sentence aroused protests by senior Allied generals, and was commuted to life imprisonment in July 1947; Kesselring was in fact pardoned and released in October 1952. Albert Kesselring died on 16 July 1960 at Bad Nauheim.

Major Helmut Lent

Born at Pyrehne on 13 June 1918, Helmut Lent was the son of a clergyman, from whom he inherited a devout religious faith and high moral values. An early passion for glider flying drew him towards a career in the air force, and in 1937 he joined the Luftwaffe. After completing his training and being commissioned Leutnant, Lent was assigned to 1 Staffel of Zerstörergeschwader 76, a wing flying the Messerschmitt Bf 110 twin-engined heavy fighter.

Lent opened his scoring right at the start of the war when on 2 September 1939 he downed a Polish PZL P.11c fighter. On 18 December two RAF Wellington bombers fell to his guns during a sortie over the German Bight; and when flying support missions during the German invasion of Norway in April–June 1940, he added five more victories. His score of eight kills qualified him as an ace, and was a respectable figure for a Bf 110 pilot – albeit achieved against Gladiator biplanes and under-

A more sombre than usual portrait photograph of Generalfeldmarschall Kesselring, taken just after the presentation of the Diamonds; his more habitual expression earned him the nickname 'Smiling Albert' from his men. Note the white Luftwaffe general officers' collar patches, with large gold wire embroidered Luftwaffe eagles over crossed marshal's batons. On his left breast he also displays Italian pilot's wings and three general's stars, in compliment to his command of Italian troops in the Mediterranean theatre.

Kesselring as commanding general of Luftflotte 2 in the West in summer 1940, wearing the Knight's Cross awarded on 30 September 1939. An artillery officer in World War I, Kesselring had a clear understanding of ground–air co-operation in the attack. He was realistic about the poor chances of an invasion of Britain unless air and naval superiority could be achieved, but in September 1940 he was nevertheless deceived by over-optimistic intelligence reports of RAF losses.

protected medium bombers rather than modern single-engined fighters. Lent was then transferred to the newly established Nachtjagdgeschwader 1, the first specialized night-fighter wing.

Helmut Lent initially hated night flying and had to be persuaded against a transfer back to day fighters. Eventually, however, he developed a real skill in this demanding role, and on 12 May 1941 he scored his first night victory; the Bf 110, by now outclassed as a day fighter, proved ideal for long night patrols free of interference from single-seaters suited to this role. By August of that year he had added 14 enemy bombers shot down on night operations to his existing eight daytime kills; and on 30 August 1941 Oblt Lent was awarded the Knight's Cross.

The kind of multiple kills that many day-fighter pilots were able to achieve during a single sortie were at this stage of the war unknown in the night interceptor squadrons, although they would later be achieved by a few aces such as Wolfgang Schnaufer (qv). However, from summer 1941 the increasing strength of the RAF night-bombing offensive, and the introduction of increasingly effective German aircraft-mounted radar, enabled Lent to build up his score steadily.

In November 1941 he was appointed Gruppenkommandeur of II/NJG 2, flying Dornier Do 215B night fighters from Leeuwarden in Holland; and by 6 June 1942, promoted Hauptmann, he had amassed a total of 35 night victories.

By January 1943 Lent's tally of night kills had reached 50; on 1 August of that year he was appointed Geschwaderkommodore of NJG 3 in the rank of Major, and the following day he was awarded the Swords, with his score of 66 night victories making him Germany's most successful night-fighter pilot. The night war over the Reich continued to grow in size and intensity, with each side making successive advances in radar interception and countermeasures; meanwhile the RAF added to the difficulties of the Nachtjagd by sending intruder fighters to hunt the hunters over their own airfields. On the night of 15 June 1944, Maj Lent was the first pilot to claim his 100th night kill; and on 31 July his achievements brought him the Diamonds, as the first night-fighter pilot to receive this award.

On 5 October 1944, flying a Junkers Ju 88, Lent took off on a routine transit flight from Stade to Nordborchen. On arrival he found that the main runway at his destination had been cratered by Allied bombers and he was forced to land on an emergency airstrip. As he brought his Junkers in to land one of the engines cut out, and the aircraft stalled, crashed and burst into flames. All four crew were thrown from the wreckage seriously injured, and the other three men died shortly after being taken to hospital. Both Lent's legs were so badly mangled that doctors

(Continued on page 41)

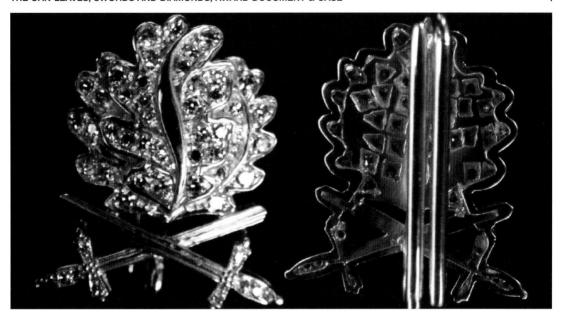

2

3

4

WOLFGANG LÜTH RETURNS FROM HIS LAST PATROL, 1943

B

HERBERT OTTO GILLE IN HUNGARY, 1945

C

COUNT STRACHWITZ BEFORE STALINGRAD, 1942

D

E

'THE GHOST OF ST TROND': WOLFGANG SCHNAUFER, OCTOBER 1944

F

G

WALTER NOWOTNY'S LAST MISSION: ACHMER, 8 NOVEMBER 1944

H

TOP LEFT **A falsified propaganda shot of the night-fighter ace Helmut Lent, supposedly as a major wearing the Oak-Leaves; an earlier photo of a notably youthful Lent has clearly been retouched to add the Knight's Cross and alter his collar patches of rank.**

TOP RIGHT **This formal portrait of Major Lent, taken at Hitler's headquarters after the award of the Swords in August 1943, is a great deal more convincing; note the obvious signs of strain on the 25-year-old pilot's face after four years of combat flying. His original Diamonds clasp was sold at auction some years ago, and is now in the collection of the Wehrgeschichtliches Museum in Rastatt.**

recommended amputation, but the chief surgeon – fearing that the shock of amputation might kill the patient – delayed the operation. However, a gangrene infection set in and amputation was Lent's only chance of survival. On 7 October 1944, Helmut Lent died on the operating table.

SS-Oberstgruppenführer u. Generaloberst der Waffen-SS Josef Dietrich

Josef 'Sepp' Dietrich was born at Hawangen on 28 May 1892. In 1911 he joined Bavarian Feld Artillerie Regt Nr 4 'König', serving with this unit through most of World War I. In June 1917 he was promoted to Vize-Wachtmeister – a warrant officer rank – and in the last months of the war he was one of the small number of German soldiers trained as tank crews.

After the war, in which he won both classes of the Iron Cross, Dietrich joined the Bavarian Police. An early member of the Nazi Party, he was also one of the first to join the new SS, becoming an SS-Sturmführer in June 1928; he served for some time as Hitler's chauffeur and bodyguard. By August 1929 he had risen to SS-Brigadeführer, and in December 1931 to SS-Gruppenführer. With this rank, in March 1933 he became commander of the SS-Stabswache Berlin, the unit which was to evolve into the 'Leibstandarte SS Adolf Hitler' (LSSAH) – the premier unit and formation in the Waffen-SS throughout World War II. As one of Hitler's most trusted lieutenants, Dietrich was personally involved in the bloody purge of the SA leadership on 30 June 1934. By the outbreak of war in September 1939 he was already an SS-Obergruppenführer (full general).

Dietrich commanded the 'LSSAH' as a motorized infantry regiment during the Polish campaign, crossing the Vistula and occupying Modlin before advancing on Warsaw. During the campaign in the West in May–June 1940 Dietrich's men were always at the forefront of the advance, but drew criticism for their recklessness and high casualties; one unit led by Wilhelm Mohnke also murdered 80 British prisoners at Wormhout. After the successful conclusion of the campaign, on 4 July 1940 Dietrich was awarded the Knight's Cross.

The 'LSSAH' was also prominent in the fast advances of the spring 1941 Balkan campaign, breaking through the Greek Metaxas Line defences and taking more than 50,000 prisoners in battle against both Greek and British Commonwealth forces. In the early phases of Operation 'Barbarossa', Dietrich's formation – now an 11,000-strong brigade – fought with Heeresgruppe Süd in the destruction of the Soviet 6th Army near Zhitomir. At Uman, Mariopol, Taganrog and Rostov the 'LSSAH' saw heavy fighting and acquitted itself well; until then the conservative Army generals had tended to sneer at the Waffen-SS as a mere political gendarmerie, but in this campaign – and particularly in the grim winter defensive battles which followed – their combat reputation was firmly established. Dietrich was awarded the Oak-Leaves on 31 December 1941.

Josef 'Sepp' Dietrich, shown here in the rank of SS-Obergruppenführer und General der Waffen-SS. The ribbon attached to his right breast pocket is for the so-called 'Blood Order' awarded to those who marched with Hitler in the abortive 1928 Munich Putsch. Despite their long personal association, in 1944–45 Dietrich was no unquestioning believer in the Führer's military competence.

In the summer of 1942 the badly mauled 'LSSAH' was withdrawn from the front for rebuilding and upgrading as a Panzergrenadier division in France; it returned to the Eastern Front in February 1943 after the disaster of Stalingrad. The division took heavy losses in the recapture of Kharkov in February–March, and Dietrich was decorated with the Swords on 14 March 1943. His division was again decimated in the battles around Belgorod and Prokhorovka during the Kursk offensive in early July; shortly thereafter Dietrich was posted back to Germany to form the new I SS-Panzerkorps. This was planned to comprise the 'LSSAH' and the newly forming 12.SS-Pz Div 'Hitlerjugend', and by early 1944 Dietrich's headquarters were in Brussels. (In the event, the corps included at various dates the 1., 2., 3. & 12.SS-Pz Divs, 17.SS-PzGren Div, and various Army divisions.)

Dietrich's corps were heavily involved in the bitter defensive and counter-attack battles following the Allied landings in Normandy in June 1944. His troops fought with great determination, but as a corps commander he himself was probably out of his depth (GFM von Rundstedt called him 'decent, but stupid'). Even so, Dietrich realized that the war could no longer be won under Hitler's leadership and, although he would not sanction any attempt on the Führer's life, he seems to have been ambivalent about radical measures short of that extreme. He was certainly fortunate that his involvement in such discussions remained unknown in the aftermath of the 20 July bomb attempt. On 1 August 1944, Dietrich was promoted to SS-Oberstgruppenführer; and five days later, in recognition of the part his troops had played in Normandy, he was awarded the Diamonds. He was briefly promoted to command 5.Panzer-armee, but most of his divisions were taken from him and squandered in the doomed counter-attack at Avranches, and he was obliged to fall back all the way across France.

In October 1944, Dietrich was appointed Oberbefehlshaber der 6.Panzerarmee; this had 1., 2., 9. & 12.SS-Pz Divs and the Army's Panzer Lehr Div, but all were greatly weakened by recent defeats. His army was committed to the northern flank of the Ardennes offensive – in December 1944, failing to reach its objectives despite early progress. In January 1945 Dietrich's battered command – soon redesignated 6.SS-Panzerarmee, and including 1., 2., 3. & 12.SS-Pz Divs – was transferred to the Eastern Front, where in March they took part in the abortive offensive around Lake Balaton in Hungary. Dietrich then carried out a fighting withdrawal into Austria, falling back from Vienna towards Krems, where on 8 May 1945 he surrendered his units to US forces.

After the war, Dietrich was tried for war crimes in respect of the shooting of US prisoners at Malmédy in the Ardennes by troops of 6.Panzerarmee. In 1946 he was sentenced to life imprisonment, reduced four years later to 25 years; he was actually released in 1955. He was subsequently re-arrested by the Germans and tried for his part in the execution of SA leaders during the so-called 'Night of the Long Knives' in June 1934; in 1957 he was sentenced to 18 months imprisonment, and was finally released in 1959.

Dietrich died on 21 April 1966, and his funeral was attended by more than 5,000 former Waffen-SS soldiers.

Dietrich was known for his mild idiosyncrasies in dress. Here he wears a fleece-lined coat, and a cap bearing a metal death's-head badge from a peaked cap beneath a hand-embroidered silver wire sleeve eagle from a tunic. In this photo he wears the old pattern collar patches for SS-Gruppenführer. Army generals with a professional staff training tended to sneer at the military ignorance of this former sergeant-major; however, they did credit him with energy, courage, and a down-to-earth, comradely attitude.

Generalfeldmarschall Walter Model

Walter Model was born on 24 January 1891 at Genthin near Magdeburg. After attending officer training school – with little distinction – he was commissioned Leutnant in 1910. He fought as a company officer with Inf Regt Nr 52 during World War I, rising to Hauptmann, and was retained in the army of the Weimar Republic. By 1935 he had reached the rank of Oberst and was serving in the Technical Department of the

Oberkommando des Heeres (Army High Command – OKH). In 1938 he was chief-of-staff of IV Armeekorps, in which post he served during the invasion of Poland. A convinced Nazi, Model became friendly with figures among the leadership; shortly before the attack on France and the Low Countries, in April 1940 he was promoted to Generalmajor and posted as chief-of-staff to 16.Armee. In reward for his performance he was given his own command, 3.Pz Div, in November 1940.

In June 1941, Model led his tank division into Russia as part of Heeresgruppe Mitte. He excelled in a field command, showing great energy and determination and winning the respect of his troops, and was awarded the Knight's Cross on 9 July. In the months that followed Model's troops fought their way past Smolesnk and, in mid September, formed part of the great pincer movement that encircled Kiev and netted huge numbers of Soviet prisoners. Promoted Generalleutnant in October, Model was given command of XLI Panzerkorps on the Upper Volga, and in January 1942 he was promoted yet again to General der Panzertruppe in command of 9.Armee – an astonishingly rapid rise. He took over his army around Rzhev in the midst of the Soviet winter counter-offensive, and proved himself just as much a master of aggressive defence as of attack. For his achievements in stabilizing the front, on 1 February 1942 he was awarded the Oak-Leaves and promoted yet again to Generaloberst.

Over the next three years, Model was regularly moved from one crisis point to another, and his tactical genius and ability to rally hard-pressed troops often saved the day. On 2 April 1943 he was decorated with the Swords. In July he led the attacks around Orel on the northern flank of the Kursk salient, commanding a total of 21 divisions in five corps. When, after initial good progress, the offensive faltered, finally to be called off in mid-July, Model commanded not only 9., but also 2.Panzerarmee for three weeks. He once again showed himself a master of defensive tactics as the Soviets began their inevitable counter-offensive, and was one of very few generals so trusted by Hitler that he was able to make tactical withdrawals on his own judgement when the situation demanded.

In late January 1944, Model was appointed Oberbefehlshaber der Heeresgruppe Nord and tasked with preventing Soviet advances into the Baltic countries; and on 1 March he was elevated to the rank of Generalfeldmarschall – at 53, Germany's youngest – with command of Heeresgruppe Nordukraine. In June 1944, Heeresgruppe Mitte reeled under the weight of the Soviet summer offensive, Operation 'Bagration', mounted with nearly 200 divisions. Model was given command, and his calming influence and supreme tactical skills enabled the tattered army group to fall back under some sort of control and stabilize a line on

Generaloberst Walter Model, wearing the Knight's Cross with Oak-Leaves. Despite the impression created by the monocle that he affected, Model did not come from the Prussian nobility family but from a fairly humble middle class background; he was one of the 'new men', who at first owed their advancement to their support of the Nazi regime. Thereafter, however, Model earned his meteoric promotion by sheer talent and determination. He was a ruthlessly demanding commander and an abrasive personality, but his troops seemed to respond to his tough, confident style.

Generalfeldmarschall Model on the Western Front in summer 1944, in conversation with Paratroop General Eugen Meindl. Model was known as the 'Führer's Fireman' due to the tendency to rush him into emergency situations, where his skills would more often than not prevent a major disaster. Immediately after more or less stabilizing the Eastern Front following the Red Army's massive Operation 'Bagration' in summer 1944, he was appointed Oberbefehslhaber West in August. Although infinitely resourceful, with the tired remnants of the armies destroyed in Normandy even Model could not halt the Allied drive across France and Belgium.

Polish territory during August. Model was a commander who inspired confidence among his troops, and never lacked it himself: when asked what reinforcements he was bringing to the crumbling central sector, his replied calmly 'Myself'. For preventing a total collapse of the central sector of the front, GFM Model was awarded the Diamonds on 17 August 1944.

That same month Model was transferred to the Western Front as Oberbefehlshaber West, in the hope that his genius for defensive warfare could hold back the advance of the Western Allies after the collapse in Normandy. There were limits to what even he could achieve, however, and within three months the Wehrmacht had been forced out of France and across Belgium and part of Holland into Germany – although troops under Model's command inflicted a heavy defeat on British airborne forces at Arnhem, and held the Scheldt estuary for many weeks. Inexplicably replaced as C-in-C West by Rundstedt, Model kept command of Heeresgruppe B; as such he had two Panzer armies – led by Dietrich and Manteuffel (qqv) – under his command for the ill-fated Ardennes offensive in December.

By spring 1945 the US armies had encircled Model's remaining troops in the Ruhr Pocket, and his pleas to be allowed to attempt a break-out eastwards were rejected. With no hope of withstanding the overwhelming Allied superiority, and no intention of being a witness to the final destruction of the regime he had served so well, on 21 April 1945 Walter Model shot himself dead.

Oberleutnant Erich Hartmann

Erich Hartmann was born at Weissach on 19 April 1922. Like many of the great fighter aces he showed an early fascination with flying, and at the remarkable age of 15 he qualified as an advanced glider pilot and instructor. Inevitably, he joined the Luftwaffe as soon as he had completed his schooling. On completion of training on powered aircraft Lt Hartmann joined Jagdgeschwader 52 on the southern sector of the Eastern Front in October 1942. He was posted to Maj Hubertus von Bonin's III Gruppe, and paired up with the experienced Ofw Rossmann to learn the rudiments of combat flying. He shot down an Il-2 Stormovik on 5 November, but it would be three months before he achieved a second kill.

By April 1943, having flown over 100 combat missions, Hartmann had scored a modest seven victories; but within another three months his number of missions had passed 200, and his tally had reached 34 victories. In August 1943, when 9/JG 52 was flying in the Kharkov region, Hartmann's score suddenly began to rocket; he shot down 49 Soviet aircraft during that month, and on the 29th he was appointed Staffelkapitän. During his year at the head of the 'Karaya' Staffel (so-called from its radio callsign), Erich Hartmann would achieve the extraordinary figure of 211 further victories.

On 20 September 1943 he scored his 100th kill – up from just seven in only five months. In October, 33 more Soviet aircraft fell victim to the 21-year-old ace, and on the 29th of that month, with his score at 148, Lt Hartmann received the Knight's Cross. (It was by now very noticeable that the high scores achieved on the Russian Front had lifted the threshold for award of the higher decorations: in 1941, 100 victories had earned Mölders the Diamonds.) After a spell of home leave Hartmann returned to his Gruppe; the unit had been driven back to the Kiev area by a Red Army advance, which in mid-January saw a Soviet tank raid destroying Bf 109s and killing groundcrew on Malaja-Wiska airfield as the Messerschmitts tried to take off. On 2 March 1944, Hartmann shot down ten aircraft, taking his score to 202 and bringing him the Oak-Leaves; on the 18th he was belatedly promoted Oberleutnant.

His Gruppe saw several last-minute moves during spring 1944 in the face of new Soviet advances: first north to Lvov in Poland, then south again to the Kherson area, then west to Romania, then north again to Minsk, and finally back to Lvov. On 4 July 1944, with his score standing at 239 victories, Hartmann was decorated with the Swords. Although the Soviet summer offensive against Heeresgruppe Mitte led to catastrophic German losses and retreats, these target-rich skies brought Hartmann one of his most successful periods: during July and August 1944 he downed 78 Soviet aircraft in just four weeks, his score passing the 250 mark on 18 July.

In the remaining months of the war Hartmann continued to increase his incredible scores; and on 23 August 1944 he reached a total of 301 kills – the first, and one of only two pilots in history to achieve 300 victories. Two days later Oblt Hartmann was awarded the Diamonds. Promoted Hauptmann, he left 9/JG 52 on 30 September to lead a new 4/JG 52 with his comrade Maj Gerhard Barkhorn's II Gruppe. Early in February 1945 he returned as Gruppenkommandeur of I/JG 52, also serving for a few days as acting commander of the co-located I/JG 53. Early in March he was ordered to report for conversion training on the new Me 262 jet fighter; but he objected strenuously to leaving his comrades behind on the rapidly deteriorating Eastern Front, and Obstlt Graf's (qv) request for his return to I/JG 52 was granted. On 17 April 1945, Hartmann was credited with his 350th kill; and his 352nd and last victim fell on 8 May – the last day of the European war.

A few days beforehand he, like his fellow 'Diamonds bearer' Hermann Graf, had been ordered to fly to Germany to avoid capture by the Soviets – and like his Kommodore, Hartmann had refused to

The greatest fighter ace of all time, Erich Hartmann was nicknamed 'Bubi' ('Sonny' or 'Kid') by his comrades because of his boyish looks. The adoring press predictably gave him more pompous labels – e.g. 'The Blond Knight of Germany' – which had a Great War ring to them.

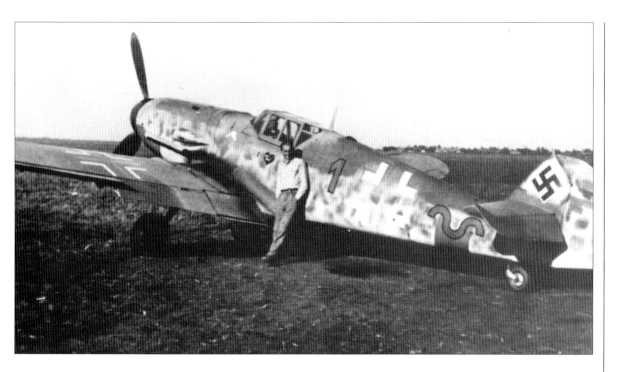

abandon his comrades. Eventually surrendering to US forces in Czechoslovakia, Erich Hartmann was handed over to the Red Army and spent ten years in Russian captivity, not being released until 1955. After the war he joined the new West German air force, where he commanded the reborn Geschwader 'Richthofen' flying the F-104 Starfighter; he rose to the rank of Oberst before retiring in 1970.

In roughly 30 months of combat flying, Erich Hartmann had flown more than 1,400 sorties, and recorded a unique tally of 352 aerial victories that is vanishingly unlikely ever to be surpassed. During the course of the war he himself had been shot down 16 times, but had always escaped major injury. A born flier and outstanding marksman, he would modestly attribute his unique success to good luck above all else. Erich Hartmann died at the age of 71 on 19 September 1993 at Weil im Schönbuch.

Hartmann posing on a Ukrainian airfield in September or October 1943 with his Bf 109G-6, bearing his markings 'yellow 1 + wavy bar' as the Staffelkapitän of 9/JG 52, and 9 Staffel's 'Karaya/ pierced heart' emblem. Just visible on the rudder are the wreathed '100' and another one-and-a-half lines of bars marking his latest victory tally.

The day after being flown to Rastenburg to receive his Diamonds at Hitler's hands on 26 August 1944 following his 300th victory, Hartmann returned to the front south of Warsaw and was photographed with his crew chief, Heinz 'Bimmel' Mertens. Hartmann often insisted upon Mertens' indispensable part in his successes.

General der Panzertruppe Hermann Balck

General der Panzertruppe Hermann Balck, in a photograph taken shortly after his investiture with the Swords in March 1943. Balck was one of Germany's most skilled Panzer leaders on both the Eastern and Western Fronts, yet his name is not widely known outside specialist circles. Unlike many senior Panzer officers, Balck did not normally wear the special uniform for tank troops but rather the regular field-grey service dress.

Hermann Balck was born in Danzig on 7 December 1893, and in February 1914 he entered the military college in Hanover as an officer cadet, being commissioned Leutnant in August of that year. After World War I he remained in the Reichswehr, and by the outbreak of World War II he was commander of Schützen Regt 1 in 1.Panzer Division.

During the May 1940 campaign Obstlt Balck earned the Knight's Cross when his unit seized a vital bridge over the River Maas north of Sedan. In August of that year he was promoted full colonel, and in mid-December was given command of Pz Regt 3 in 2.Panzer Division. With his new command, Obst Balck took part in the invasion of Greece in May 1941. Just after the invasion of the Soviet Union began the following month, Balck was attached to the OKH and tasked with ensuring availability of the motor vehicles essential for the campaign. In reward for his success in this post he was appointed General (Inspekteur) der Schnelltruppen, though still with the rank of Oberst, in November 1941.

Balck returned to a combat command in May 1942 when he was given 11.Pz Div, which he led with great distinction, achieving a record when his Panzers destroyed 91 Soviet tanks in one day of combat. Promoted to Generalmajor in August 1942, Balck took part in the drive to the Caucasus with Heeresgruppe Süd, and was awarded the Oak-Leaves on 20 December 1942. Shortly thereafter Balck was promoted to Generalleutnant, and in March 1943 was awarded the Swords after his troops annihilated an entire Soviet Shock Army in the Caucasus. Following the Allied landings at Salerno in Italy that summer Balck was posted to command XIV Panzerkorps, but he was seriously injured when his spotter plane crashed, and he was placed on the reserve.

In November 1943, Balck was promoted to General der Panzertruppe and posted back to the Eastern Front to take command of XXXXVIII Panzerkorps. In furious defensive fighting around Kiev, Zhitomir, Berdichev and Brusilov, Balck once again proved himself a field commander of the highest order; in the latter battle his corps destroyed the Soviet 60th Army.

In August–September 1944, Balck commanded 4.Panzerarmee with great success during the Soviet summer offensive against Heeresgruppe Mitte; his troops halted a breakthrough into Poland, then counter-attacked and drove their opponents back to their starting point with heavy losses. For this achievement, on 31 August 1944 he was awarded the Diamonds. During the following month he was given command of Heeresgruppe G on the Western Front, where in actions around Metz his armoured force – which could muster only 30 tanks – halted an American attack with over 700 tanks, destroying more than a third of the US force. His tactics were simple but ingenious: he had dummy minefields prepared, which the US troops soon detected, advancing overconfidently into genuine minefields.

Balck spent the closing weeks of the war back on the Eastern Front, in command of 6.Armee fighting near Budapest. Late in March 1945 he reported to OKW that his troops were losing the will to fight, and were concerned only to avoid encirclement. Gradually retreating westwards, Balck and his army surrendered to the Americans in Austria early in May.

After being released from captivity in 1947, Balck moved to Stuttgart; however, in 1948 he was charged with ordering the execution of an artillery officer in November 1944 – Balck had ordered the officer shot when on the eve of an operation he was found to be drunk and incapable and had no idea of the location of his own guns. Balck was sentenced to three years' imprisonment, but released after 18 months. Hermann Balck died in 1982 at the age of 89.

General der Fallschirmtruppe Hermann Bernhard Ramcke

Ramcke was born in Schleswig on 24 January 1889. His military career began not as a soldier but as a trainee seaman, serving as a ship's boy in the Imperial Navy in 1904–07. He saw pre-war service on several warships, and after the outbreak of World War I on the cruiser *Prinz Adalbert*. In 1915–16 he fought ashore in Flanders with Matrosen Regt Nr 2, rising to the rank of Feldwebel. Seriously wounded, he spent 18 months in hospital; but he returned to the front in 1917, fighting with the Marine Sturmabteilung, and before the end of the war he survived another wound and rose to the rank of Leutnant.

After commanding a company in the Freikorps von Brandis – and taking a third wound – Ramcke transferred to the post-war Reichswehr as a Haupt-mann in 1919, becoming a platoon commander in Infanterie Regiment 1. Among his inter-war postings was command of the troop training grounds at Gross Born. An Oberstleutnant commanding an infantry regiment at the outbreak of World War II, he joined the staff of 7.Flieger Div and attended Fallschirmschule III at Braunschweig in July 1940, qualifying for his jump badge in August. On 1 August, Obst Ramcke officially transferred to the Luftwaffe, being posted to the staff of Fallschirmjäger Regt 3 and shortly afterwards to FJR 1, where he formed heavy weapons units. In 1941 Ramcke took over the recruitment, reserve and training units of the airborne troops formation XI Fliegerkorps.

During the attack on Crete in May 1941 he commanded the Luftlande Sturm Regt, landing with his troops at Maleme airfield. In recognition of his part in Operation 'Mercury', Ramcke was promoted Generalmajor in July and awarded the Knight's Cross on 21 August 1941. After some months attached to the Italian Army assisting with the formation of the 'Folgore' Parachute Division, Ramcke was posted to North Africa in April 1942 to command Fallschirm Brigade 1. In October 1942, when the Axis line at El Alamein collapsed under the pressure of Gen Montgomery's offensive, Ramcke's brigade was cut off in the southern desert; he led them for 80 miles to catch up with the retreating German army, in the process capturing a British convoy and freeing some 100 Italian and German prisoners. For this achievement he was decorated with the Oak-Leaves on 13 November 1942, and on 21 December he was promoted to Generalleutnant.

Generalmajor Hermann Bernhard Ramcke, shortly after the award of the Oak-Leaves in November 1942 for his leadership of a paratroop brigade cut off in the desert after El Alamein; he wears Luftwaffe tropical uniform, having been summoned from North Africa to receive his award personally from Hitler. This remarkable officer spent years in each of the three armed services. After joining the Imperial Navy as a boy seaman in 1904, he saw heavy fighting and repeated wounds with the naval infantry in Flanders in World War I, rising through the ranks to gain a commission and both classes of the Iron Cross. After transferring to the Army in the interwar years, and later to the Luftwaffe, he qualified as a paratrooper at the age of 51 in 1940.

Major Heinz Wolfgang Schnaufer, seen here wearing a late-war leather flying jacket with broad velveteen collar, under a life preserver; his Knight's Cross with Oak-Leaves, Swords and Diamonds is displayed at his shirt collar. The son of a wealthy wine merchant, Schnaufer returned to run the family business after the war. He was on a wine-buying trip to France in 1950 when his sports car was involved in a fatal collision, and he died at the age of 28.

In mid-February 1943, GenLt Ramcke was tasked with forming the new 2.Fallschirmjäger Div, of which he was to become commander. In September 1943, when the Italian government concluded a separate armistice with the Allies, 2.FJ Div was flown to Rome to disarm Italian troops, and subsequently made a few limited parachute jumps in the Mediterranean theatre; but that month Ramcke was hospitalized, not returning to duty until February 1944. That April, after a spell fighting in the Ukraine, his 2.FJ Div returned to Britanny to refit. Elements fought the Allied landings in Normandy in June; and on 11 August, Ramcke was appointed as commander of 'Fortress Brest'. His isolated garrison held out until 20 September; during the siege Ramcke was promoted General der Fallschirmtruppe, and on the day before the capitulation he was awarded both the Swords and the Diamonds simultaneously.

Eventually taken to a POW camp in the USA, he twice escaped – not in hope of reaching neutral territory, but in order to draw public attention to the mistreatment of German prisoners (such ill-treatment, leading in some cases to death, is now well documented). In December 1946, Gen Ramcke was handed over to the French, who in 1951 charged him with alleged war crimes; but this attracted such levels of international protest that he was quickly released. Hermann Bernhard Ramcke died in retirement at Kappeln on 5 July 1968.

Hauptmann Heinz Wolfgang Schnaufer

Wolfgang Schnaufer was born in Stuttgart on 16 February 1922, into the family of a wealthy wine merchant. After completing his education at an NPEA school (National Political Educational Establishment – Nazi-sponsored schools for the academically gifted who intended a career in the military), he entered the Luftwaffe in November 1939. On completing flying training in 1941 he volunteered for night fighters, and in November 1941 was posted to II Gruppe of Nachtjagdgeschwader 1 at Stade, south of Hamburg.

Schnaufer's first operational sortie came in February 1942, when his Gruppe was assigned to fly night cover for the *Scharnhorst, Gneisenau* and *Prinz Eugen* during the so-called 'Channel Dash' when the German heavy cruisers broke out from Brest to sail for Norwegian waters. It was not until 1 June 1942 that Schnauffer scored his first aerial victory, however, when he shot down an RAF Halifax bomber over Belgium. His score rose only very slowly; by the end of the year, despite being officially an ace, he had scored only seven kills – though three of these had been achieved in a single night on 1 August 1942. Promoted Oberleutnant in July 1943, Schnauffer became Staffelkapitän of 12/NJG 1 based at Leeuwarden in the Netherlands; at that point his score stood at 17 victories.

However, his successes now began to mount up more rapidly; he was credited with his 42nd kill in December 1943, when he was awarded the Knight's Cross. He remained at Leeuwarden until March 1944, when he was appointed Gruppenkommandeur of IV/NJG 1 and the unit moved to St Trond in Belgium. Schnaufer was promoted to Hauptmann in May 1944; the following month, after his tally reached 84 victories, he received the Oak-Leaves. Two months later, with a score of 89, Schnauffer was awarded the Swords, and at the same time his two regular crewmen received the Knight's Cross (for most of his combat missions his radar operator was Fritz Rumpelhardt and his gunner Wilhelm Gansler). On 9 October 1944, following his 100th victory, Schnauffer was awarded the Diamonds.

The advance of the Allied armies across the Low Countries in autumn 1944 forced the withdrawal of the night-fighters to Germany. In November, Schnaufer was appointed Kommodore of NJG 4; in December, still aged only 22, he was promoted Major, and by the end of the year his score had reached 106 kills. Major Schnaufer continued to fly combat missions until the end of the war, and despite all the difficulties of flying operations over the collapsing Reich his successes continued to mount; on the night of 21 February 1945 he shot down ten RAF heavy bombers. At the end of the war in May his confirmed kills stood at 121 (though another, from his rampage on 21 February, was only confirmed after the war, making his total 122).

Taken prisoner by the British in May 1945, he was released later that year and took over the management of the family business. On 13 July 1950 he was mortally injured in a car accident, and died in hospital from head injuries two days later.

The Luftwaffe's two leading night-fighter aces: Helmut Lent (left) and Wolfgang Schnaufer (see Plate F), photographed together some time in early 1944. Between them these two young officers destroyed 233 Allied aircraft over Western Europe; Lent was already an ace before transferring from Bf 110 day fighters, but Schnaufer spent his whole combat career in night fighters.

Fregattenkapitän Albrecht Brandi

Albrecht Brandi was born on 20 June 1914 in Dortmund. He joined the Kriegsmarine in 1935 as an officer cadet, serving as watch officer on a minesweeper. By the outbreak of war Brandi had been commissioned Leutnant zur See, and served on surface ships engaged in anti-submarine duties in both the Baltic and North seas. He was promoted Oberleutnant zur See on 20 May 1940, commanding the minesweeper M1 until April 1941, when he transferred to the U-boat service and began his training for submarines.

Brandi was fortunate enough to serve his apprenticeship on the Type VIIC boat U-552 under a leading U-boat ace, Erich Topp. In April 1942 he was given his own Type VIIC, U-617; and on 7 September 1942 he scored his first success when he sank a small steamer – *Thor II*, of just 300 tons. More worthwhile successes followed just two weeks later, when he encountered a small convoy and in quick succession sank the *Athelsultan* (8,800 tons), the *Tennessee* (2,300 tons) and the *Roumanie* (3,600 tons). Brandi was promoted to Kapitänleutnant on 1 October 1942.

At the beginning of November 1942, Brandi was ordered to take his boat through the tightly guarded Straits of Gibraltar and into the dangerous waters of the Mediterranean. This was a far more confined

This formal 1943 photograph shows Albrecht Brandi as a Kapitänleutnant just after the award of his Oak-Leaves. Brandi's career was unusual in two respects: he was one of only a small number of U-boat commanders to see service in the dangerously shallow waters of the Mediterranean, and to be credited with sinking a significant number of warships among his tally of victories.

and hazardous theatre of operations for U-boats than the Atlantic, with a number of powerful British naval bases; and while convoys in these waters were often smaller, they were also far more heavily protected, since they consisted mainly of vital war supplies for the British forces in North Africa and on Malta. Undeterred, on one occasion Brandi attacked a large single transport ship escorted by no less than five warships; and on another he attacked the British battleship HMS *Rodney*, also protected by a large escort. However, it should be noted that during one patrol Brandi had lined U-617 up for a perfect shot on a fast-moving transport only to realize at the last moment that it was a hospital ship, at which point he broke off his attack.

On 21 January 1943, Brandi was awarded the Knight's Cross. On 1 February he scored a major success when he torpedoed and sank the British minelaying cruiser HMS *Welshman*; while most U-boat commanders avoided warships wherever possible, Brandi deliberately sought them out. His Oak-Leaves followed barely three months after his Knight's Cross, and he acquired the reputation of being an expert in this sort of action.

In the late summer of 1943 Brandi was specifically tasked with locating and attacking a powerful British battlegroup consisting of a battleship and two aircraft carriers which had been reported east of Gibraltar. On 9 September, Brandi found himself watching the carrier HMS *Illustrious* through his periscope, but try as he might he was unable to work himself into a good firing position due to its speed and its constant zig-zagging. Deprived of his main target, Brandi turned on her escorts, and with a spread of four torpedoes he sank the destroyer HMS *Puckeridge*. The British lost no time in putting up air patrols to track down the U-boat, and on 12 September U-617 was attacked and damaged by bombs. She managed to limp into Spanish waters, where the crew was interned.

On orders from Adml Dönitz, however, Brandi was smuggled out of Spain by German agents and brought safely back to Germany. In January 1944 he took command of a new Type VIIC boat, U-380, but she was badly damaged in an air raid before he could take her to sea. In April 1944 Brandi took command of another Type VIIC, U-967, again for operations in the Mediterranean. Since the Allied victories in North Africa and Sicily the previous summer these were quite extraordinarily hazardous waters for German shipping; yet in the months that followed Brandi added yet another warship, the destroyer USS *Fechteler*, to his tally. On 9 May 1944, Brandi was promoted to Fregattenkapitän, and on the same day was awarded the Swords.

Brandi was subsequently transferred to a shore posting, as commander of U-boats operating in Finnish waters. On 24 November 1944 he was decorated with the Diamonds. At the end of that year, at his own request, Brandi was transferred to take command of the so-called

Kleinkampfverbände. These units operated with 'one-man torpedoes', midget submarines, assault motorboats and other small craft. Brandi's final tally had been 115,000 tons of enemy shipping sunk, and as well as 20 merchant ships that total included three Allied cruisers, an incredible 12 destroyers and a minesweeper.

After the war Brandi enjoyed a successful career as an architect. He died on 6 January 1966 in his native Dortmund.

Generalfeldmarschall Ferdinand Schörner

Born in Munich on 12 June 1892, Schörner saw a great deal of combat as a junior officer with Bavarian units during World War I, both on the Western Front and in Italy where – like Rommel (qv) – he won the Pour le Mérite for gallantry at Caporetto in October 1917. Schörner spent some time in the Freikorps movement before returning to Army service, but by 1937 he had reached the rank of Oberstleutnant, commanding Gebirgsjäger Regiment 98.

On the outbreak of war in September 1939, Obst Schörner's mountain riflemen took part in the assault on the Polish fortress of Lvov (Lemberg) with 1.Gebirgs Division. In August 1940 he was promoted Generalmajor, to form the new 6.Gebirgs Division. His division saw intensive action during the campaign in the Balkans, taking part in the breakthrough of the Metaxas defence lines – which were overrun in just 24 hours – and on 27 April 1941 his troops raised the German flag over the Acropolis. For his achievements in the Greek campaign Schörner was decorated with the Knight's Cross on 20 April.

Schörner's division formed part of Armeekorps Dietl during the attack on the Soviet Union in June 1941, in action on the far northern sector of the front in the ultimately unsuccessful drive towards Murmansk. On 27 January 1942, Schörner was promoted to General-leutnant and given command of XIX Gebirgskorps. He spent the next two years fending off innumerable Soviet attacks in this northern sector, gaining a reputation as an extremely tough commander who was the terror of rear-echelon types, but gave every consideration to hard-pressed troops in the front lines, where he was often to be seen himself. In June 1942 he was promoted to General der Gebirgstruppe.

On 1 October 1943, Schörner was given command of XXXX Panzerkorps on the Dnieper river in the southern sector of the front. Here once again he proved himself in defensive actions against superior enemy forces, demanding the greatest efforts from his men but gaining their respect. Mentioned in despatches for his part in the defence of the Nikopol bridgehead, he was awarded the Oak-Leaves on 17 February 1944, and promoted to Generaloberst on 1 March. A convinced Nazi, he was also appointed head of the National Socialist Political Guidance Corps.

Appointed to command Heeresgruppe Südukraine, Schörner, like Model, was one of the few senior commanders Hitler trusted to make tactical withdrawals on his own judgement; he used this freedom fearlessly, yet was never punished or called to account for it. When given responsibility for the defence of Odessa in the summer of 1944, he realized that his position was untenable and withdrew his troops over the Dnieper, sacrificing Odessa but stabilizing the front and saving his entire army group from certain defeat.

Schörner was then transferred back to the north on 21 July 1944, arriving with Heeresgruppe Nord in time to face yet another enemy offensive. With only two armies (16. & 18.) and a small number of independent brigades, Schörner held off ten times as many Soviet divisions, earning himself the Swords on 28 August 1944. He then made a fighting withdrawal into Latvia; but a determined Soviet thrust to Memel cut off more than 27 German divisions in the Kurland peninsula in October. In the months that followed Schörner once again mounted a spirited defence, and under his command the German forces in Kurland beat off four major Soviet offensives.

On 1 January 1945, in recognition of his achievements in Kurland, Schörner was awarded the Diamonds, and shortly thereafter he was entrusted with Heeresgruppe A (later retitled Mitte), trying to defend a 300-mile line from Poland down into Czechoslovakia with the mauled remnants of some 24 divisions. He did what he could to hold off the advancing Red Army; aware of what lay in store for German territory occupied by the Soviets, he insisted on absolute determination and obedience, to buy time for the civilian population to evacuate westwards. On 5 April 1945, Ferdinand Schörner was promoted to Generalfeldmarschall, the last German ever to achieve this rank.

Generalfeldmarschall Ferdinand Schörner, wearing the traditional *Bergmütze* cap of the mountain troops. Below the Knight's Cross he displays the Pour le Mérite ('Blue Max') that he won at the battle of Caporetto on the Italian front in October 1917, when this veteran of Verdun was a platoon commander in one of the two Bavarian battalions of Jäger Regiment 3 in the Imperial Army's Alpenkorps. (Josef Charita)

Schörner continued to resist the Soviet advance south of Berlin, and in the closing days of the war he was ordered to lead his troops to the so-called 'Alpine Redoubt' in Bavaria. This never actually existed; he eventually left his command and flew westwards to surrender to US troops in the Tyrol. This desertion made him unpopular, and did not save him; he was promptly handed over to the Soviets. Remarkably, despite his Nazi sympathies, they attempted to persuade him to turn to communism and become a general in the East German Army. When he refused he was sentenced to 25 years' imprisonment.

In the event Schörner was released in 1955, and returned to Germany. In 1957 he was charged over the deaths of several German servicemen executed on his orders for desertion or defeatism in the closing days of the war. He was sentenced to four and a half years' imprisonment, but released after two. Ferdinand Schörner, the last surviving German Generalfeldmarschall, died on 2 July 1973 in Munich.

General der Panzertruppe Hasso von Manteuffel

Hasso von Manteuffel was born in Potsdam on 14 January 1897, into an aristocratic family with a long tradition of military service. In February 1915 he joined Husaren Regt Nr 3 as an officer cadet, receiving his commission in April 1916 and earning both classes of the Iron Cross before the war ended.

After a spell with Freikorps von Oven he joined the Reichswehr in 1919, and in the inter-war years he became well known in the world of equestrian sports. By the outbreak of World War II he had left the cavalry, and was serving in the rank of Oberstleutnant as an instructor with the Panzer school at Berlin-Krampnitz.

Just before the invasion of the Soviet Union, Manteuffel requested and was given command of a motorized infantry battalion with 7.Pz Div, showing great personal courage and dash in fierce fighting at Smolensk and Vyazma. In August 1941 he took command of Schützen Regt 6 in the same division, and fought around Rzhev and Klin. Promoted to Oberst in October, he then led a battlegroup which seized a vital bridge over the Volga–Moskova Canal, a position that Stalin himself had ordered be defended to the last. For this courageous achievement Manteuffel was awarded the Knight's Cross on 31 December 1941.

In early 1942 Manteuffel came near to being court-martialled when he took his troops out of their designated positions to pursue a fleeing enemy unit, but the fact that they succeeded saved him. Through early 1942 Manteuffel led his division's motorized infantry brigade, until they were withdrawn to France for rebuilding in May. In February 1943, Obst von Manteuffel was transferred to North Africa, taking command of a scraped-together division of paratroopers, Panzergrenadiers and Italian Bersaglieri during the last hopeless battles in Tunisia.

A formal portrait of Schörner wearing the Oak-Leaves with Swords and Diamonds, at the collar of a piped service tunic. His typically unsmiling features remind us that he was often regarded as a brutal commander; however, although he could be pitiless towards any man who was not doing his utmost, he made more allowances for fighting soldiers than for rear-echelon personnel.

Exhausted and ill, he was evacuated to hospital in Germany, and on 1 May 1943 he was promoted to Generalmajor. On his recovery three months later he returned to the Eastern Front, where he took command of his old 7.Pz Div on the southern sector of the front, facing the determined Soviet offensives which followed the failure of Operation 'Citadel' around Kursk in July. He distinguished himself once again in the recapture of Zhitomir, and on 23 November 1943 he was awarded the Oak-Leaves.

At the end of 1943 Manteuffel's achievements were further rewarded by command of the elite 'Grossdeutschland' Division, the best-equipped Panzergrenadier formation in the German Army. In February 1944 he was promoted Generalleutnant, and retrospectively awarded the Swords for his command of 7.Pz Div in the closing months of 1943. Under his leadership the 'GD' distinguished itself in battle – though at great cost – at Korsun (Cherkassy), in Besserabia, at Pruth and at Jassy in Romania, usually against far superior Soviet forces. Promoted to General der Panzertruppe on 1 September 1944, Manteuffel was appointed to command 5.Panzerarmee on the Western Front.

After a setback in Lorraine, his new command was rebuilt to take part in the ill-fated Ardennes offensive of December 1944, with Panzer Lehr,

2. & 116.Pz Divs, and 18., 62. and 560.Volksgrenadier Divisions. Allocated the central axis of advance, his army was distracted by the failure of 7.Armee on their left flank to take Bastogne, and from Christmas onwards the clearing weather brought massive Allied air intervention. 5.Panzerarmee captured St Vith on 21 December; but by 9 January 1945 the German fuel and ammunition reserves were exhausted, and all the committed forces were forced to retreat. Nevertheless, for his part in the successful early phase of the offensive and for his long and distinguished service Gen von Manteuffel was awarded the Diamonds on 18 February 1945.

In March 1945, Manteuffel took command of 3.Panzerarmee, attempting to halt the Soviet advance through Pomerania. With precious little fuel and very few tanks still remaining, his forces were gradually pushed westwards. Manteuffel ignored orders to strike towards Berlin, in the knowledge that this would result in the pointless destruction of his remaining troops. Instead he allowed his divisions to continue westwards, to surrender to the British who were approaching Mecklenburg.

Released after two years' captivity, Manteuffel became active in German politics, and from 1953 to 1957 was a member of the Bundestag for the Free Democratic Party. His political career came to an end when he was charged with having ordered the execution of a soldier who deserted his post, but a sentence of two years' imprisonment was quashed by President Theodor Heuss. General von Manteuffel remained a popular and respected figure; he lectured at the US Military Academy at West Point, and was invited to the Pentagon and also to the White House to meet President Eisenhower. Hasso von Manteuffel died during a holiday trip to Austria on 24 September 1978.

Generalmajor Theodor Tolsdorf

Theodor Tolsdorf was born at Oletzko on 3 November 1909, and in 1934 he joined Infanterie Regiment 1. He was commissioned Leutnant in 1936, and subsequently posted to Inf Regt 22 of 1. Inf Div based at Gumbinnen. Promoted Oberleutnant in October 1938, he became a platoon leader in the regiment's 14th (Anti-Tank) Company, and served in this capacity during the Polish campaign of September 1939, winning the Iron Cross in both classes.

Tolsdorf missed the campaign in the West as his unit was being re-formed; however, he did see considerable combat during the opening phases of Operation 'Barbarossa' in summer 1941. Wounded in action during the push towards Leningrad, he insisted on returning to his unit at the front before his wounds were fully healed, and was awarded the Knight's Cross on 4 December 1941. Shortly afterwards Tolsdorf was severely wounded once again, and lost his right foot. After being fitted with a prosthetic he returned to active service once more, now a Hauptmann in command of I Bataillon of his regiment, still with 18. Armee in the north. Promotion to Major followed in 1943, when he was appointed to take command of his regiment. Tolsdorf was awarded the Oak-Leaves on 15 September 1943 for his outstanding leadership, the award being personally presented by Hitler in a ceremony at the *Wolfsschanze*.

His division now transferred to Heeresgruppe Süd, and shortly after returning to the front Maj Tolsdorf was wounded in action yet again, being hit in the stomach; while being evacuated for treatment he was

ABOVE **Generalmajor Hasso von Manteuffel in a formal study taken shortly after his award of the Oak-Leaves in November 1943, when he was commanding 7.Pz Div on the Eastern Front. Manteuffel was greatly respected by all ranks for his courageous leadership; as a motorized infantry battalion commander in summer 1941, he had led his men into at least one audacious assault with rifle in hand.**

BELOW **General von Manteuffel – known as 'the Panzer Baron' – photographed wearing the black 'special uniform for tank crews' following his decoration with the Diamonds in February 1945. He wears the death's-head collar patches which were regulation on this uniform for all ranks, but his officer's version of the black Panzer field cap has gold piping for a general officer.**

wounded once more, this time in the head. After recovering from his wounds Tolsdorf was posted as a tactics instructor to the Metz officer candidates' training school. Promoted to Oberstleutnant, he returned to the northern sector of the Russian Front once again in March 1944, taking command of Gren Regt 1067 which was tasked with defending Vilnius, Lithuania. Soviet units had already bypassed the city, and Tolsdorf first had to break through to the beleaguered garrison – rescuing on the way a field hospital with more than 3,000 German wounded. Tolsdorf defended the city until a relief force from 3.Panzerarmee under GenObst Reinhardt arrived. For this achievement Tolsdorf – christened the 'Lion of Vilnius' by the propagandists – was awarded the Swords on 18 July 1944, and promoted to Oberst on 1 August.

At the end of 1944, Obst Tolsdorf was given command of 340.VolksGren Div for the Ardennes offensive; promotion to Generalmajor would follow on 30 January 1945. As part of I SS-Panzerkorps his division seized and held a river crossing, for which operation he was awarded the Diamonds on 18 March 1945, and on 1 April 1945 he was promoted Generalleutnant. Tolsdorf was then given command of LXXXII Armeekorps in the Balkans; he ended the war there – at 35 the youngest soldier of his rank in the Wehrmacht – and managed to ensure that his troops were taken prisoner by US rather than Soviet forces.

After his release from captivity in 1947, Theodor Tolsdorf returned to a more modest career as a driver. Following a serious accident in which he suffered a double skull fracture, he died on 1 June 1978 in Wuppertal.

Oberst Theodor Tolsdorf, wearing the Swords awarded for his defence of Vilnius in March 1944. This fearless and much-wounded infantry officer, whose name is unknown even to most students of World War II, ended the war as the youngest lieutenant-general in the Wehrmacht and the holder of his country's supreme award. After the war he worked as a truck driver.

General der Panzertruppe Dr Karl Mauss

Karl Mauss was born on 17 May 1898 at Plön. He first saw combat at the age of just 16 years as an officer cadet, and was the first – and youngest – soldier in his unit to win the Iron Cross Second Class. Within a year he had been commissioned Leutnant, and by the end of World War I he had added the First Class to his awards. In the difficult years after the war he earned a living as a newspaper seller, before studying dentistry; he qualified in 1929, but rejoined the military in 1934.

After the outbreak of World War II, Mauss, now a Major, saw action in Poland and the West with 4.Pz Div; and in the rank of Oberstleutnant he distinguished himself in the invasion of the USSR, when the division fought as part of Heeresgruppe Mitte. Mauss was awarded the Knight's Cross on 26 November 1941 and was promoted to Oberst; in January 1942 he served briefly as acting divisional commander when Gen von Saucken (qv) was wounded in action. The 4.Pz Div took part in the drive to the Caucasus in 1942, and in the northern pincer of the Kursk offensive, around Orel, in July 1943; thereafter it saw heavy defensive fighting around Gomel. Oberst Mauss was decorated with the Oak-Leaves on 24 November 1943.

On 31 January 1944, Mauss was appointed as commander of 7.Pz Div, and was confirmed in this post and promoted to Generalmajor on 1 April. This division had taken heavy losses west of Kiev the previous November; it continued to fight on the defensive during the retreat across the northern Ukraine in spring 1944, and against the Soviet summer offensive against Heeresgruppe Mitte, before being transferred north to the Baltic states in August under 3.Panzerarmee. There it fought in Lithuania, Kurland and around Memel until November 1944. Mauss was promoted to Generalleutnant on 1 October, and awarded the Swords on 23 October 1944.

His division was again heavily committed during the Soviet offensive between the Vistula and the Oder in January–March 1945; during this Pomeranian campaign GenLt Mauss was severely wounded on 22 March and subsequently had a leg amputated. He was evacuated to East Prussia; and on 15 April he was awarded the Diamonds.

After the war, Dr Maus returned to dentistry. He died on 9 February 1959 in Hamburg.

General der Panzertruppe Dietrich von Saucken

Dietrich von Saucken, the last soldier to be awarded the Diamonds, was born on 16 May 1892 at Fischhausen, the son of a magistrate from an old and distinguished family. He served in the cavalry in World War I; and by the outbreak of World War II, Obst von Saucken held the command of Reiter Regiment 2. He led his regiment in the Polish campaign, before transferring to command the Schützen Brigade (motorized infantry) of 4.Panzer Division.

During Operation 'Barbarossa' the division advanced into the USSR under Heeresgruppe Mitte, with which it would be continuously engaged for nearly three years. Oberst von Saucken was wounded in action during the crossing of the Dnieper; but on 27 December 1941, still in the rank of Oberst, he took over command of 4.Pz Div just as the German advance was running out of steam. During the savage winter defensive fighting he was successful in blocking the advance of an enemy corps to the north of Orel; in recognition of his successful leadership he was promoted to Generalmajor on 1 January 1942, but almost immediately he was seriously wounded once again. On 6 January, Saucken was awarded the Knight's Cross as he recovered from his wounds.

On his release from hospital, Saucken took command of the Army's Panzer training school at Berlin-Krampnitz, and in this appointment he was promoted to Generalleutnant on 1 April 1943. Thereafter he

Oberst Dr Karl Mauss after the formal presentation of his Oak-Leaves in late 1943; the badge over his left breast pocket is the Close Combat Clasp for personal participation in close-quarter fighting over a number of days. As commander of 7.Pz Div in Pomerania early in 1945, GenLt Mauss would be seriously wounded and would lose a leg. Like the more famous GenMaj Dr Franz Bäke, who ended the war with the Oak-Leaves and Swords as commander of 13.Pz Div (see Elite 133), Dr Mauss was a dentist by profession, and returned to his practice after the war.

returned to command 4.Pz Div on 31 May 1943, in time to take part in the huge armoured offensive at Kursk. When Operation 'Citadel' failed and the Soviets launched their counter-offensive, Saucken's vigorous leadership of his division frustrated a Soviet pincer movement against 9.Armee; for this achievement, on 22 August 1943 GenLt von Saucken received the Oak-Leaves. His division became involved in repeated defensive actions that autumn to thwart Soviet attempts to force a wedge between 2. and 9.Armee, and they eventually halted a Soviet force estimated at ten times their strength near Kalinkovichi. On 31 January 1944, Saucken was awarded the Swords.

Briefly appointed to command III Panzerkorps in June 1944, he was given XXXIX Panzerkorps at the end of that month, and led it until mid-October 1944. This formation fought under 4.Armee with Heeresgruppe Mitte during the fighting withdrawal in the face of the Soviet summer offensive, and almost as soon as Saucken received his command it suffered heavy losses when encircled east of Minsk. The corps later retreated westwards through Kurland and East Prussia, and Saucken once again proved himself an expert tactician, launching surprise counter-attacks on Soviet spearhead units. His corps finally came to a halt near Memel on the Baltic coast, and on 1 August 1944 he was promoted General der Panzertruppe. The next major engagement for XXXIX Panzerkorps was in northern Poland, where Saucken's troops temporarily halted Soviet attempts to force their way through a gap between 3.Panzerarmee and Heeresgruppe Nord, destroying hundreds of enemy tanks in the process.

In December 1944, Gen von Saucken was given command of the new Panzerkorps 'Grossdeutschland', which effectively consisted only of the mechanized division of that name, recently evacuated by sea from the Memel bridgehead to East Prussia. Between mid-January and mid-March 1945 the 'GD' was forced back towards Königsberg and into the Balga peninsula, before its remnants took ship again, back to Schleswig-Holstein.

On 12 March 1945, Gen von Saucken was given command of 2.Panzerarmee with the impossible task of holding the coastal area around Gotenhafen, Danzig and Hela against Gen Rokossovsky's 1st Belorussian Front, advancing from the south; this region was teeming with frantic German civilian refugees, and Hitler had ordered it to be held to the last man. Following a Soviet breakthough towards Gotenhafen, Saucken ignored his suicidal orders and, with the help of the Kriegsmarine, rescued as many civilians as possible before evacuating 40,000 of his men by sea to the Putzinger Spit. There he took command of the new Heeresgruppe Ostpreussen, a combination of the remnants of 2.Panzerarmee and 2.Armee. Tasked now with defending the area around Fischerhäuser Bay and the Frische Nehrung, his weak forces held out gallantly as desperate attempts were made to evacuate as many of the 300,000 civilian refugees as possible.

It was in this command that on 8 May 1945, the last day of the war, Gen von Saucken was informed that he had been awarded the Diamonds by GrAdml Dönitz, the nominal head of state after Hitler's suicide. Dönitz had sent an aircraft to evacuate Saucken, but the general refused to abandon his troops, and went into Soviet captivity with them.

The last soldier to win the Diamonds, awarded to him on the very last day of the European war, Dietrich von Saucken was an aristocratic cavalry officer who later became a highly skilled Panzer general. After leading 4.Pz Div and two Panzerkorps including the 'Grossdeutschland', he was appointed to command of an army, and served with particular distinction in defensive operations on the Eastern Front. These two photos from slightly different angles show the scarring left by his serious head wound. Although his sufferings in Soviet captivity left him confined to a wheelchair, Gen von Saucken lived to the age of 88. (Josef Charita)

Saucken was held for ten years in Siberian prison camps, often in appalling conditions; his health never recovered, and thereafter he was confined to a wheelchair. After his return to Germany he devoted himself to an earlier interest in painting, and became a successful artist. The last of the *Brillantenträger*, Dietrich von Saucken died on 27 September 1980 at Pullach, at the age of 88 years, and was buried with full military honours.

THE PLATES

A: THE OAK-LEAVES, SWORDS AND DIAMONDS, AWARD DOCUMENT & CASE

1 The obverse and reverse of the first pattern Oak-Leaves with Swords and Diamonds clasp. The basic format closely follows that of the standard Oak-Leaves with Swords, and this first pattern clasp is significantly smaller than the second pattern. The reverse view shows the strengthening rib around the edges, and the manner in which the clasp is drilled out to allow better reflection of light through the stones. (William Eicher Collection via Gary Mott)

2 The obverse and reverse of the second pattern clasp, by Klein of Hanau; the shape and format are significantly different from the first type. Note in the reverse view that the swords are cast as two separate pieces; and the central leaf is a separate piece, riveted to the underlying leaves – one of the rivet heads is visible on the reverse at the 7 o'clock position. Visible just below the hilt of the right-hand sword is the Klein logo of a circled letter 'K'. This is the actual piece awarded to Helmut Lent, and now in the collection of the Wehrgeschitchtliches Museum in Rastatt. (Courtesy Detlev Niemann)

3 The actual vellum award document or Urkunde for the 'Diamonds' is held within a leather-bound frame with gold tooled decoration. The national emblem, and all the lettering, are in gold leaf. This example, awarded to Werner Mölders, was photographed for a Third Reich propaganda magazine before it was passed to Hitler for signature.

4 The outer face of the case for the Urkunde. For a Luftwaffe recipient, it is covered in blue-grey leather; and note that the swastika within the wreath clasped by the eagle of the national emblem is set with small diamonds. All of the metallic embellishments are fire-gilded.

B: WOLFGANG LÜTH RETURNS FROM HIS LAST PATROL, 1943

On his return to Bordeaux in autumn 1943 from his extended second cruise in the South Atlantic and Indian Ocean, Korvettenkapitän Lüth of U-181 is greeted by Kapitän zur See Hans Rudolf Rösing, Führer der U-Boote West, after his extraordinary 205 days at sea – the second longest ever war cruise. For her return to harbour the crew of this Type IXD boat had evidently repainted part of the conning tower the better to display the total tonnage sunk during both of U-181's Indian Ocean patrols – 105,812 tons. They also rigged wires to fly victory pennants, one for each ship sunk; but on this occasion, realizing that it would be their captain's final war cruise, they flew a pennant for each ship sunk during his entire combat career – 46 in all.

Although almost completely bald-headed, on this voyage Lüth grew a positively luxuriant 'ginger' beard. He is dressed in an ordinary seaman's boarding cap; a khaki tropical shirt, with a seaman's yellow-on-khaki right breast eagle, but his shoulder boards of rank (equivalent to an Army major); he

displays his Knight's Cross with Oak-Leaves and Swords, to which the Diamonds were added on 9 August 1943. A pair of faded denim trousers and canvas-and-rubber shoes complete his outfit. Lüth and his crew attended a boisterous party at the 12th Flotilla base before visiting the barbershop.

C: HERBERT OTTO GILLE IN HUNGARY, 1945

This plate reconstructs a photo taken of SS-Obergruppenführer und General der Waffen-SS Gille when he was commander of IV SS-Panzerkorps in Hungary in winter 1944/45, in conversation with one of his divisional commanders, SS-Brigadeführer Hellmuth Becker of 3.SS-Panzer Division 'Totenkopf'. Like many senior figures in the Waffen-SS, Gille affected several personal variations on regulation uniform and insignia (although the carved walking stick was a traditional item carried by many German commanders in the field). Such liberties were widely tolerated, particularly in highly decorated soldiers.

His M1943 field cap, with officers' piping and insignia, was modified with a deep fold-down flap faced with dark fleece. The collar of the coat that he wore in place of the regulation greatcoat seems to be faced with short, dark fur. This re-cut, shortened watchcoat, with hand-warmer pockets over the ribs, bears no sleeve eagle, but does display his shoulder boards of rank: interwoven gold and silver cord on a dove grey-over-black underlay, with two silver stars. Gille's tunic

RIGHT **Generalleutnant Hasso von Manteuffel (see Plate E) in 1944, wearing either a tropical olive-brown or a lightweight reed-green field uniform, with his old style field cap; he displays the Oak-Leaves with Swords awarded in February 1944 under the button-down shirt collar. (Josef Charita)**

collar rank patches show three oak-leaves and two stars, in silver on black; and he wears the Knight's Cross with Oak-Leaves, Swords and Diamonds. Gille owed his Diamonds to his determined defence of and successful break-out from the 'fortress' city of Kovel against Gen Rokossovsky's 1st Belorussian Front in spring 1944. On his left tunic sleeve and thus invisible here, Gille normally wore a 'Wiking' cuff title hand-embroidered in Gothic rather than the regulation Latin script. Over their riding breeches both Gille and Becker wear Luftwaffe fleece-lined flying boots against the cold of mid-winter. Becker wears regulation uniform, apart from the boots and his cuffband; this has the old death's-head badge of the pre-war Totenkopf Standarte Oberbayern, rather than the divisional title.

D: COUNT STRACHWITZ BEFORE STALINGRAD, 1942

This plate is taken from a photo of Oberstleutnant Hyazinth Graf Strachwitz, commander of Panzer Regiment 2, 16. Panzer Division, in the turret of his command tank in October 1942. During the advance on Stalingrad by 6.Armee, GenMaj Gunther Angern's 16.Pz Div was a spearhead of the northern pincer, achieving several notable successes and being the first formation to reach the River Volga. Strachwitz is pictured wearing his famous personal cap – the Panzer officer's black *Feldmutze* with regulation piping and insignia, but modified with a facing of black astrakhan ('Persian lamb') all around the flap. He also had a fur collar facing added to his regulation field-grey greatcoat; greatcoats were widely used by tank crews in the Russian winter, despite their awkward bulk. The junior officer standing waiting for orders is lucky in having received one of the first sets of the new padded, reversible grey/white winter clothing, which arrived in winter 1942/43 and for which motorized troops seem to have enjoyed priority.

Judging by its cupola and hatch, the tank in the original photo appears to be a PzKw IV F2, still finished at this date in the original dark grey, with white-bordered red turret numbers; the '01' of the regimental commander's tank is clearly shown in the photo.

E: HASSO VON MANTEUFFEL IN ROMANIA, MAY 1944

Generalleutnant Hasso von Manteuffel, the 'Panzer Baron', is illustrated here from photographs taken in Romania in late spring 1944, when he was commanding the Panzergrenadier Division 'Grossdeutschland'. In March the division had been pushed back across the Dneister river and into Romania, where it fought in April around Jassy, before again withdrawing behind the River Prut. In May the weakened division enjoyed a brief respite and received some new equipment before launching a counter-offensive towards Jassy in June. Here, GenLt von Manteuffel is visiting his artillery regiment; his Kfz 1/20 Schwimmwagen field car, 'WH-1637813' – note divisional commander's pennant – was driven by a Panzer Obergefreiter. Manteuffel wears his habitual 'old style officer's field cap', with gold general officer's piping and hand-embroidered gold bullion badges instead of the regulation flat-woven type. He was often photographed wearing the issue rubberized coat for motorcyclists. Beneath it he wears no tunic in the spring heat, just a button-collar shirt displaying his Knight's Cross with Oak-Leaves and Swords. Major Krieg, commanding the Panzer Artillerie Regiment 'GD', was photographed wearing a soldier's tropical field cap and a lightweight reed-green tunic; his insignia are conventional, except that he displays on his right sleeve a badge for single-handed destruction of a tank.

F: THE 'GHOST OF ST TROND': WOLFGANG SCHNAUFER, OCTOBER 1944

In October 1944, Major Wolfgang Schnaufer, commanding IV Gruppe, Nachtjagdgeschwader 1 at St Trond, Belgium, achieved his 100th aerial victory by night, and on the 9th of that month he was awarded the Diamonds. The number of night victories required for the higher awards was much lower than for day fighter pilots, but the Nachtjagd mission was much more difficult. Schnaufer's aircraft at that date is illustrated here: a late model Messerschmitt Bf 110G, finished dark grey on upper surfaces and pale blue on side and undersurfaces, with low-visibility NJG 1 code 'G9' and larger individual aircraft letters 'EF'. (By this stage of the war the rigid fourth-letter sequence for Gruppe Stab flights and Staffeln seems to have broken down; officially, the final 'F' would indicate a V Gruppe Stab machine.) The aircraft is fitted with FuG 202 SN2 radar, and an upwards-firing *Schrage Musik* mounting for twin 20mm cannon in the rear cockpit, in addition to the four nose cannon; Schnaufer reckoned that he achieved about half his kills with this weapon, flying below his targets. (Throughout his operational career Schnaufer only flew the Bf 110.) A detail of his tail fin tally shows the arrangement of aircraft silhouettes, RAF roundels, and dates; he often achieved multiple victories on

Hauptmann Erich Hartmann in September 1944, in the cockpit of a Bf 109G bearing the famous 'Karaya/ pierced heart' emblem of his 9 Staffel, III Gruppe, JG 52 (see Plate G).

single nights – e.g. while flying as Kommodore of NJG 4 on 2 February 1945 he shot down nine bombers, and ten on the 21st of that month. The other detail shows the badge of NJG 1 painted below the cockpit on the port side.

The portrait shows Maj Schnaufer wearing regulation Luftwaffe officer's service uniform, with shoulder boards and collar patches of his rank on the golden-yellow underlay of the flying branch. His awards are the Iron Cross Second Class (buttonhole ribbon) and First Class (left breast); the German Cross in Gold (right breast), and his Knight's Cross with Oak-Leaves, Swords and Diamonds (throat). He also displays a Mission Clasp in gold for 100 missions (above left pocket), and below it the Pilot's Badge and a silver Wound Badge. Schnaufer was also photographed in the late-model heated leather flying jacket, with a tailored waist and broad dark blue velveteen collar.

G: THE ACE OF ACES: 'BUBI' HARTMANN, HUNGARY, WINTER 1944/45

On 30 September 1944 the newly promoted Hauptmann Erich Hartmann was transferred from command of 9.Staffel in III Gruppe, JG 52, and took over a newly formed 4/JG 52 in II Gruppe. While the other two Gruppen of the Geschwader were rushed north to East Prussia, Maj Gerhard Barkhorn's II Gruppe fought the Red Air Force over Hungary, based at Budaörs. One of the aircraft flown by Hartmann at that time is illustrated: a Messerschmitt Bf 109G-6, with late-production clear-view cockpit canopy but not yet with the taller tail fin. White '1' and a bar indicate the Staffelkapitän of the first Staffel in a II Gruppe. There is no Geschwader insignia, just Hartmann's famous personal decoration of a black 'tulip' around the nose. When he left 9/JG 52 he had to leave behind its 'Karaya/ pierced heart' Staffel badge; but he kept the heart itself, marked with his fiancée Ursula Paetsch's nickname 'Usch' in Gothic letters (top detail patch). The more famous form of his 9/JG 52 marking is shown below (second detail patch); 'Ursel' was an alternative nickname for the same girl.

Hartmann was often photographed, and his extravagantly crushed service cap was something of a trademark. Here a dark blue-grey shirt sets off the Diamonds he was awarded for passing 300 aerial victories on 24 August 1944. Flying jackets were often private-purchase items, and many photos of Hartmann show this black leather example. Other photos of the period show him in a dark blue-grey cloth regulation K So/41 jacket, with white-on-dark-blue Hauptmann's rank patches on both sleeves, worn together with riding breeches and flying boots, a field belt, compass, and holstered Walther PPK.

H: WALTER NOWOTNY'S LAST MISSION: ACHMER, 8 NOVEMBER 1944

On the overcast morning of the 8th, Maj Nowotny waits impatiently for mechanics to fix the fault in his Me 262A-1a so that he can fly his first combat mission against USAAF bombers. His plane, WNr 110400, bears the narrow yellow belly-band used by Kommando Nowotny as a recognition sign, and the 'white 8' which he had often used on his Bf 109s and Fw 190s; the yellow forward nacelles also seem to have been a personal recognition sign. Overhead, only Lt Franz Schall has managed to 'scramble', from the nearby runway at Hesepe; he will account for two US fighters. Schall's Me 262 (WNr 170047, 'white 1' and 'S') is painted differently from Nowotny's plain dark green fighter, having two-tone splinter camouflage over all upper and side surfaces. Schall would fly again that afternoon with Nowotny, but lost sight of his CO when they climbed through thick cloud; he claimed two Mustangs before one of his engines failed, and he managed to bale out. Nowotny did not, and died when his Me 262 came out of the clouds in a vertical dive. His shooting down is tentatively credited to Lt Edward Haydon, a Mustang pilot of the USAAF 357th Fighter Group, and possibly shared by Capt Ernest Fiebelkorn of the 20th Fighter Group. We reconstruct Nowotny wearing his unstiffened service cap and grey leather coat from photographs, over standard K W/41 winter flying trousers and flying boots.

Walter Nowotny receives his Diamonds from the hands of the Führer at Rastenburg; the formal portrait photo showing him wearing the new award (see page 20) would be taken later that day.

INDEX

Figures in **bold** refer to illustrations.

Afrikakorps 16–17
airforce, award recipients 5–16, 19–21, 22–5, 30–2, 41, 45–7, 50–1
army, award recipients 16–18, 22, 26–7, 29–30, 43–5, 48–9, 53–60

Bagration, operation 44–5
Balck, Gen d.Pan Hermann (1893–1982) **48,** 48–9
Barbarossa, operation 6, 29, 42, 56, 57, 58
Becker, SS-Brigaf Hellmuth **C**(35), 61, 62
Bittrich, Willi 17
Bölling, Fw **25**
Brandi, Fregkap Albrecht (1914–1966) 51–3, **52**
Britain, Battle of 5, 7–8

'Channel Dash', the 9, 50
Condor Legion 5, 6

Dammers, Fw Hans **15**
Dietrich, SS-Obstgruf Josef 'Sepp' (1892–1966) 17, 41–3, **42, 43**

Fallschirmjäger, award recipients 49–50
Focke-Wulf Fw jet fighter **10**
France, Battle of 5, 7, 16, 44

Galland, GenLt Adolf (1912–1996) 6–10, **7, 8, 9, 10,** 21
Gille, SS-Gruf Herbert Otto (1897–1966) 27–9, **28, C**(35), 61–2
Gneisenau (battle cruiser) 9, 50
Golden Oak-leaves with Swords and Diamonds clasp award 24
Gollob, ObstLt Gordon (1912–1987) 10–12, **11,** 21
Göring, Reichmarshall Herman (1893–1946) **4,** 6, 8, 9
Graf, Obst Hermann (1912–1988) **14,** 14–16, **15**

Hartmann, OLt Erich 'Bubi' (1922–1993) **G**(39), 45–7, **46, 47, 62, 63**

Hitler, Adolf (1889–1945) **4,** 16, 17, 28, **63**
Hube, GenObst Hans Valentin (1890–1944) 29–30, **30**

Junkers Ju 87 dive bomber 23, **25**

Kesselring, GFM Albert (1885–1960) 30–1, **31**
Knight's Cross of the Iron Cross *see* Oak-leaves with Swords and Diamonds clasp award
Kriegsmarine, award recipients 18–19, 51–3

Leibstandarte SS Adolf Hitler 41, 42
Lent, Maj Helmut (1918–1944) 31–2, 41, **41, 51**
Luftwaffe, award recipients 5–16, 19–21, 22–5, 30–2, 41, 45–7, 50–1
Lüth, Kap z.*See* (1913–1945) 18–19, **19, B**(34), 61

Maldinger, Uffz **25**
Manteuffel, Gen d.Pan Hasso von (1897–1978) **E**(37), 54–6, **56, 61,** 62
Marseille, Hptm Hans Joachim (1919–1942) **12,** 12–14, **13**
Mauss, Gen d.Pan Dr Karl (1898–1959) 57–8, **58**
Mertens, Heinz 'Bimmel' **47**
Messerschmitt Bf 109 fighter **13, 47**
Messerschmitt Me 262 jet fighter 10, 21, **21**
Model, GFM Walter (1891–1945) **33,** 43–5, **45**
Mohnke, Wilhelm 42
Mölders, Obst Werner (1913–1941) **5,** 5–6, **6**
Montgomery, Gen Bernard 17, 49

navy, award recipients 18–19, 51–3
'Night of the Long Knives' 41, 43
Normandy defences 17, 42
North African campaign 16–17, 49
Nowotny, Maj Walter (1920–1944) 19–21, **20, H**(40), 63, **63**

Oak-leaves with Swords and Diamonds clasp award

description 3–4
documentation **A3**(33), 61
first pattern (Godet) **A1**(33), 61
forgeries of **3**
golden version 24
presentation case **A5**(33), 61
second pattern (Klein) **A2**(33), 61
Oesau, Hptm Walter **6**

paratroop, award recipients 49–50
Prinz Eugen (battle cruiser) 9, 50

Ramcke, Gen d.Fal Herman Bernard (1889–1968) **49,** 49–50
Rommel, GFM Erwin (1891–1944) **16,** 16–18, **17, 18**
Rudel, ObstLt Hans Ulrich (1916–1982) **4,** 22–5, **23, 24, 25**
and unique gold version of award 24
Russian campaign 22, 26–7, 28–9, 29, 30, 42, 44, 45–6, 48, 53–4, 55–6, 56–7, 57–8, 58–9

Saucken, Gen d.Pan Dietrich von (1892–1980) 58–60, **60**
Scharnhorst (battle cruiser) 9, 50
Schnaufer, Maj Heinz Wolfgang (1922–1950) **F**(38), 50, 50–1, **51,** 62–3
Schörner, GFM Ferdinand (1892–1973) 53–4, **54, 55**
Schulz, Obst Adalbert (1903–1944) 22, **22**
Spanish Civil War 5, 6
Strachwitz, GenMaj Hyazinth Graf (1893–1968) **26,** 26–7, **27, D**(36), 62
Süss, Ofw Ernst **15**

Tolsdorf, GenMaj Theodor (1909–1978) 56–7, **57**

U-boats 18–19, 51–3

Waffen-SS, award recipients 27–9, 41–3
Wehrmacht, award recipients 16–18, 22, 26–7, 29–30, 43–5, 48–9, 53–60
Wormhout killings 42

Zwerneman, Ofw Joseph **15**

Related Titles

Visit the Osprey website

- Information about forthcoming books

- Author information

- Read extracts and see sample pages

- Sign up for our free newsletters

- Competitions and prizes

www.ospreypublishing.com

To order any of these titles, or for more information on Osprey Publishing, contact:

Osprey Direct (North America) *Toll free:* 1-866-620-6941 *Fax:* 1-708-534-7803 *E-mail:* info@ospreydirectusa.com

Osprey Direct (UK) *Tel:* +44 (0)1933 443863 *Fax:* +44 (0)1933 443849 *E-mail:* info@ospreydirect.co.uk

www.ospreypublishing.com

The history of military forces, artefacts, personalities and techniques of warfare

Full colour artwork

Unrivalled detail

Photographs

Knight's Cross with Diamonds Recipients

1941–45

On 28 September 1941, Hitler instituted a new, supreme class of the Knight's Cross decoration for gallantry and leadership: the Oak-Leaves with Swords and Diamonds. This award would be presented to only 28 soldiers, sailors and airmen, out of the approximately 15 million who served in the German armed forces. This title describes and illustrates all 28 of those men – from fighter aces and U-boat commanders, to the youngest generals in the Wehrmacht, and field marshals in command of army groups – and including one officer for whom Hitler had to invent a literally unique award that set him apart even among the 'Diamond-bearers'.

US $17.95 / $25.95 CAN

ISBN 1-84176-644-5

OSPREY
PUBLISHING

www.ospreypublishing.com